TEACHING KINDERGARTEN : A DEVE

DATE DUE

SE 16 94 / NO 26 97			
MR 1 '96			
MY 3 '96			
NO 24 '97			
MR 13 98			
OC 27 99			
AP 24 00			
OC 15 01			
NO 15 00			
DE 6 01			
DE 19 01			
NO 18 '02			
MY 21 '03			
NO 15 06			

Teaching Kindergarten

Teaching Kindergarten
A Developmentally Appropriate Approach

Copyright © 1992 by:

Bonnie Brown Walmsley
Anne Marie Camp
Sean A. Walmsley

HEINEMANN
Portsmouth, NH

he world

Page 3, Figure 1-1: These are taken from a pamphlet, containing a talk given by Mrs. John Kraus-Boelte to the National Education Association in Baltimore, July 10th, 1876. The pamphlet is not copyrighted.

Library of Congress Cataloging-in-Publication Data
Walmsley, Bonnie Brown.
    Teaching kindergarten : a developmentally appropriate approach / Bonnie Brown Walmsley, Anne-Marie Camp, Sean A. Walmsley.
        p. cm.
    Includes bibliographical references.
    ISBN 0-435-08715-0
    1. Kindergarten—United States—Methods and manuals.
I. Camp, Anne-Marie.   II. Walmsley, Sean A.   III. Title.
LB1169.W26 1991   92-8496
372.21'8'0973—dc20   CIP

Printed in the United States of America
Printed on acid free paper
92 93 94 95 96 97 10 9 8 7 6 5 4 3 2 1

Contents

Preface

This book is a result of many years spent in early childhood education. We have worked with children aged three through eight years in a variety of settings. Bonnie Walmsley has taught Head Start in Roxbury, Massachusetts; kindergarten, first, and second grade in upstate New York. Anne Marie Camp began her teaching career at a day-care center in the Bronx, New York. From there she moved to Newburgh, where she taught kindergarten in an inner-city school. Later, she taught kindergarten in Ballston Spa. She also was director of a day-care center in Saratoga Springs. The origins of this book lie in Bonnie's first experiences teaching kindergarten in 1984, in the same suburban school district where she taught first and second grade. From the start, she found the traditional kindergarten program severely limiting and mostly inappropriate for a modern kindergartner. Excited by the work of educators such as Carol Chomsky, Charlotte Huck, Frank Smith, Donald Graves, and David Elkind, she began to change her curriculum towards what is now called a developmentally appropriate approach. Anne Marie Camp joined Bonnie in 1988, and they have been sharing a classroom ever since, Bonnie teaching the morning class, Anne Marie the afternoon. The program described in this book is jointly planned but separately taught by the two authors.

Sean Walmsley has spent the last fifteen years teaching and researching in the Reading Department at the State University of New York at Albany. He specializes in the theory and practice of integrating language arts at the elementary level; for the past ten years, he has been working closely with a number of schools in upstate New York, Massachusetts, and Vermont, helping teachers rethink their K–8 language arts and content-area programs.

We have tried to present our program in a way that would be helpful to teachers seeking alternatives to traditional approaches, be they experienced kindergarten teachers or just beginning to teach at this level. When we first started teaching kindergarten, what we wanted were teaching ideas, not philosophical treatises on early education. Unfortunately, many of the books we read gave us great ideas, but only for a single lesson, or an elegant philosophy from which we were expected to create our own lessons. Consequently, we have deliberately provided very specific teaching routines, including teaching guides. As we became more comfortable with our teaching routines, we began to reflect on the "why" of teaching kindergarten: these reflections are contained in chapter 1. We hope our reflections—and our teaching strategies—will stimulate even experienced kindergarten teachers.

Wherever possible, we have suggested techniques and approaches that can be used in a variety of kindergarten settings, with different sized classes, with varied kinds of programs (half-day, full-day), and with different kinds of students. Of course every situation is different, but we have tried to provide enough detail so that teachers can try out the routines and then adapt them to their own situation.

In this book we explain our teaching philosophy and our program. In chapter 1 we briefly review the history of kindergarten and explain what we think a kindergarten program ought to strive for and why. Chapters 2 and 3 describe the major elements of our program and how they fit together: in chapter 2 we show how the program is organized physically; in chapter 3 we describe the daily routines. Chapter 4 is devoted to the content of our curriculum; we don't teach subjects in the traditional way, but we do expect that our children will gain useful knowledge of science and history, and grow in their numeracy, literacy (reading, writing, speaking, listening), aesthetic, and physical abilities. In this chapter we explain what kinds of knowledge and skills we hope our children will develop and how we weave these subjects into our themes and daily routines. In chapter 5 we explain our approach to evaluation and give examples of the ways in which we assess our children's progress, and report to parents and our school district.

In a separate book *Teaching Kindergarten: A Theme-Centered Curriculum,* we provide detailed daily schedules for the themes we use in our program, listing the activities and resources we use for these themes.

Although we have made everything look quite neat and tidy for the purpose of this book, we know the reality of working with young children isn't so neat and tidy. Many days go by where we are unable to follow our plans—the Nurse is screening for vision and hearing and we are continually interrupted by groups of children filtering in and out. Donald has had a bad weekend at home and comes to school out of sorts and unwilling to cooperate in any way. A thunderstorm stirs up outside and the children are frightened by and preoccupied with the thunder and lightning. There are some days when plans and themes need to fall by the wayside while we tend to the more immediate needs of the children. That's fine with us. A curriculum has to be flexible and accommodating if it's to survive and thrive.

We know from our own and other teachers' experiences that making the transition to a developmentally appropriate approach is a difficult, time-consuming, and often frustrating process. We wrote this book so that others who follow the path we have taken will find it less difficult to follow, yet equally challenging and rewarding.

Acknowledgments

We'd like to thank all the students and parents that we've worked with throughout the years, but we are particularly indebted to the class of 1991, who gave us permission to videotape and to use examples of their work in this book. Thanks are also due to Superintendent Ed McHale, Jr., Assistant Superintendent James Cioffi, and the Board of Education of Shenendehowa Central Schools for their support and encouragement, and their official approval of this project. We have also benefited greatly from the assistance of colleagues and staff in Arongen School, where we teach: our thanks to Sue Rogers, Peter Merchant, Brigitte Altwicker, and Louise Cowan, who helped us search for good literature, and to Dr. Richard McDonald, Principal of Arongen. We are also in debt to colleagues with whom we have worked over the years and from whom we have learned so much: Carol Parker, Janet Sansone, Pat Mastroianni, Richard Allington, Anne McGill-Franzen, Ginny Sipperly, Elsie Cagle, Trudy Walp, Walter S. Millman, and Laure Skutt.

During the writing of this book and its companion volume, *Teaching Kindergarten: A Theme-Centered Curriculum*, we took advantage of the considerable talents of Mary Alice and Peter Amidon, and consequently were able to gather a wide variety of traditional and contemporary songs for the program. We also gained from the expertise of the University at Albany's

Educational Communications Center, where Johnnie Angus's skills in editing videotape were particularly appreciated.

We are especially grateful to Philippa Stratton, Editor-in-Chief at Heinemann, who had confidence in our original proposal for a book on kindergarten; to Cheryl Kimball, Production Editor, and to her able colleagues (Tom Seavey, Julie Hahn, Susan Mesner, to name a few) who so carefully and cheerfully guided us through the painstaking process of translating our beliefs and experiences into print; and to Mary Sims, who illustrated both this book and the curriculum guide.

As every writer knows, writing books takes precious time away from one's family. From Anne Marie, thanks to Brendan, Sarah, and Laura for their constant support and humor; from Bonnie and Sean, thanks to Katharine and Jonathan for their forbearance (it's bad enough having one parent working on a book, but when both are...).

Finally, we need to acknowledge the many sources we have used over the years to guide our thinking and planning. These are referenced in the bibliography, but we have made a special list, in Appendix C, of the books that have been most useful to us—ones we think other teachers will find helpful in moving toward a developmentally appropriate approach to kindergarten.

Bonnie Walmsley
Anne Marie Camp
Sean Walmsley
Upstate New York
January 1992

History and Philosophy of Kindergarten

1

It is hard to imagine, looking back to the colonial period from the vantage point of the 1990s, that the prevailing philosophy in the eighteenth century regarding the education of the very young was that children were innately depraved, and that their only hope of salvation lay in their growing up in an atmosphere of fear and discipline (Weber, 1969). In 1762, Jean Jacques Rousseau wrote a book, entitled *Emile*, on the education of young children, which departed radically from the prevailing philosophy. The first words of the book were: "God makes all things good; man meddles with them and they become evil" (quoted in Blenkin & Kelly, 1981). From Rousseau we can trace the beginnings of child-centered early education; indeed, from Rousseau flows the entire progressive education movement. In 1837, Friedrich Froebel founded the first kindergarten—a term Froebel himself coined and the one we still use today. Very little of Froebel's kindergarten pedagogy survives, but his legacy includes more than nomenclature. The principles upon which Froebel based his kindergarten—a strong conviction that children were innately good and that the kindergarten curriculum should be child-centered (that is, based on the child's developmental needs rather than on society's expectations for what it wanted children to know)—still prevail in modern conceptions of kindergarten. But from Froebel's first kindergarten to our own,

1

the purpose of kindergarten, its pedagogy, and its curriculum have been continually, and at times bitterly, debated.

A Brief History of Kindergarten

A brief excursion into the history of kindergarten* not only reveals something about the underlying tensions that exist between different approaches to kindergarten, but also provides the basis for the balanced approach to kindergarten we take in this book. It will also demonstrate that what we propose as appropriate kindergarten activities are not new—they derive from practices in use, in some instances, for over a hundred years.

Froebel's philosophy of kindergarten can be summed up in his own words: "The great aim and end of the whole enterprise is the education of a person from the earliest years through his own doing, feeling, and thinking and in conformity with his own nature and relationships so that his life is an integrated whole. This will be achieved if the child's activity is rightly fostered and his essential nature developed and experienced.... Not only the child's material environment but also everything which happens to him must express its reference to a higher unity of life" (Lilley, 1967, p. 119).

At the center of Froebel's kindergarten were what he called *gifts* and *occupations*. The gifts comprised a variety of precisely dimensioned balls, cylinders, cubes, blocks, lines, rings, and sticks for the children to manipulate and play with, in a particular order and in very specific combinations. The occupations comprised a variety of activities, using both the gifts and other materials. For example, children could fold and cut paper in geometric designs, make mats by weaving, lay sticks according to particular designs, and interlace paper strips to form patterns.

---

*The history of kindergarten is a fascinating subject, and we cannot do it justice in this brief review. Kindergarten teachers who want to discover their roots, so to speak should read one or more of the several excellent books and articles on this topic. We especially recommend Weber (1969), Ross (1976), and Spodek (1982) for their insightful historical analyses, and McGill-Franzen (in press), whose book puts these historical developments into a public policy framework. We also recommend reading original (or translations of) books and pamphlets written by the early kindergarten pioneers (these are readily available in larger libraries). The writing style of these early educators is often rather dense and ornate, but their writings are well worth the effort to obtain and read. Very little of what we do today is not thoroughly grounded in the philosophy, theory, and practice of educators who literally created the field of early childhood education over a hundred years ago. We owe them a great debt.

Pricking, or perforating (one of Froebel's "occupations")

Pea-work (connecting small corks with wire)

FIGURE 1–1

Other occupations included pea-work (joining sticks and peas), pricking or perforating (making figures by piercing squared paper with pins), sewing, drawing, and modeling in clay (Figure 1-1). The gifts and occupations formed the core of the program, but there were other important aspects, too. Froebel considered it important that children care for animals and plants, and so there was a real garden connected with each kindergarten in which children would plant and take care of flowers and vegetables (Kraus-Boelte, 1876). Froebel himself assembled a collection of stories, verses, songs, pictures, mottoes, and finger and movement plays for mothers to use with their young children, but these were also used in the kindergarten to introduce children to the world of literature. He also described, in detail, a variety of games and movement plays designed to develop all parts of the body as well as the senses. "These games are representations from nature—its life and human occupations; they are more or less dramatic and are accompanied by songs relating the story of action" (Kraus-Boelte, 1876, p. 17). Many of these movement plays were to be done with the children in circles so as to emphasize the sense of community and belonging, a principle that underlies most of Froebel's techniques.

Froebel's kindergarten was first introduced to the United States by Margaretha Schurz in 1849. While the movement was slow in starting (there were less than twelve kindergartens in the United States in 1870), it spread rapidly in the 1870s, and by 1880 there were more than four hundred across the country (Weber, 1969). While educators such as Elizabeth Peabody and Susan Blow embraced Froebel's educational philosophy, many found solace in the kindergarten's ability to deal with the oppression of poor children and to promote good child-rearing practices amongst poor parents. Thus, the kindergarten became popular as a means for social reform, and indeed it spread rapidly outside the framework of public education, through what were called Free Kindergarten Associations. The utilitarian aspects of Froebel's program (the *occupations*) were especially liked because they offered vocational training for children in slum areas (Weber, 1969).

While it was inevitable that Froebel's kindergarten program would be modified by American practitioners, what really brought about changes in his techniques were a succession of challenges and modifications, around the turn of the century, to the principles on which Froebel based his kindergarten (Ross, 1976). The psychologist G. Stanley Hall, for example, had done studies of children's development that raised questions about the desirability of having children sit for long periods of time doing activities with small objects that required fine-motor control (for example, sewing and perforating). John Dewey, while drawn to Froebel's use of play activities, was not happy with Froebel's belief in absolute truth; "in Dewey's pragmatic philosophy, ideas were not fixed, but changed with varying circumstances and as new bases for thinking developed" (Weber, 1969, p. 51). Indeed, Dewey's criticism of Froebel's techniques strikes at the heart of Froebel's teacher-controlled environment, where children were required not only to work with abstract concepts but also were unable to initiate their own activities (they simply imitated the teacher's models). Dewey even refused to use the term kindergarten, calling it instead the *sub-primary* curriculum. Edward L. Thorndike, whose findings on the efficacy of stimulus-response in teaching and learning were later to have far-reaching effects on the kindergarten curriculum, argued that kindergarten teachers would be better off "stimulating the formation of acceptable habits and to inhibit inappropriate ones" (Weber, 1969, p. 54).

These criticisms prompted variations on the Froebel kindergarten. For example, Dewey's sub-primary program emphasized realistic tasks of home, work, and community rather than the abstract gifts and formal occupations. In fact, the entire approach to kindergarten was to build a mini-community in which children learned how to become citizens by being citizens.

G. Stanley Hall's criticisms led to programs in which *free play* (children being encouraged to play with whatever they chose) replaced the gifts and occupations. Weber (1969) describes a prize-winning kindergarten program at the turn of the century that is organized around the theme of Abraham Lincoln, and its gifts and occupations involve not the original Froebel concepts but Lincoln-related activities.

What are?

By 1907 there were deep rifts between kindergarten educators, and at meetings of the International Kindergarten Union, the debates between orthodox Froebelians and the reformers drew large audiences. An effort in 1907 to resolve these differences resulted in a report that spelled out three approaches—one that presented what was by now the conservative Froebel program; one that offered a liberal alternative, drawn heavily from Dewey's educational philosophy; and a third, very brief, description of a compromise between the two.

Not long after this, another early childhood program emerged from Europe, this time from Italy, devised by Maria Montessori. She had established a school for retarded children in 1900 and another for "normal" children in 1907. In 1909, she began a training course for educators based on her book, now called *The Montessori Method* (Montessori, 1964). In 1915, she was invited by the National Education Association to give a talk in the United States, and she remained in the country, giving courses on her approach until 1918 (Hainstock, 1986). Unfortunately for both her and her method, William Kilpatrick and others had visited Montessori schools in Europe and issued highly critical reports, which were most likely responsible for the cool reception that Montessori received in this country. Also, Maria Montessori's insistence that teachers rigidly follow her techniques came at a time when many kindergarten educators were beginning to break away from Froebel's prescriptive routines. When reintroduced in the late 1950s by Nancy Rambusch (Rambusch, 1962), Montessori's methods were much more warmly received, and there has been a strong, if modestly sized, Montessori presence in early childhood education ever since. But even today, the movement is split between the more orthodox Montessori educators and those who have liberalized the approach (Hainstock, 1986).

There are several aspects of the Montessori method that contrast quite sharply with the Froebel approach. One is that activities were designed for individual children, not groups of children. Another, expressed in the Montessori doctrine of *liberty*, is that children should have freedom to use the materials provided in the program in their own way: "Development cannot be taught... we leave the children free in their work, and in all actions that are not of a disturbing kind" (Maria Montessori, quoted in Hainstock, 1986, p. 63). A third difference lies in the practical life exercises, in which children learn to care for themselves and their environment (these have much in common with Dewey's realistic tasks for home and community). The fourth aspect is the sensorial exercises, which are designed to develop the child's five senses and lay the foundation for speech, reading, writing, and arithmetic. (It was these sensorial activities that most offended the Froebelians in 1914.) As with Froebel, however, Montessori presented a paradox: on the one hand, she championed the cause of individual choice and the absence of teacher control; on the other, she provided a prepared environment in which children were highly restricted with respect to their thinking. She was also criticized for introducing reading and writing skills (thought by many to be inappropriate for children of this age), while denying children exposure to literature.

During the period immediately before and after the First World War, according to Weber (1969), kindergarten educators assimilated the various theories and approaches, and a number of changes occurred. G. Stanley Hall's point about the inappropriateness of fine motor activities such as sewing and perforating, led to free play with larger objects (for example, large blocks, which to this day are a staple part of the kindergarten program). Stories about everyday life began to be read to children, slowly competing with classical literature and moralistic tales, a trend that has continued to this day. Kindergarten educators also began to think about the content of the kindergarten curriculum—in other words, the knowledge kindergartners should acquire. In 1919, Alice Temple suggested that the kindergarten curriculum should focus on three content areas: (1) natural objects and phenomena—*nature study*; (2) human beings and human activities—*home and community life*; and (3) the products of human intelligence—*literature, music, and art.* William Kilpatrick, who had earlier criticized Montessori's approach, developed one of his own, the Project Method, in which the entire curriculum was organized around different kinds of projects:

practical (building a boat, putting on a play); aesthetic (listening to stories, appreciating pictures, problem solving, finding out whether dew falls); and knowledge-based (learning a specific skill). Alice Krackowizer (1919), in a book entitled *Projects in the Primary Grades*, laid out a comprehensive scheme for a kindergarten program that included detailed lesson plans on such projects as planting gardens and making dolls' furniture. (She would have heartily approved of our theme-based approach; in many ways, our themes are modern versions of her projects.)

Character training, always a principal aim of kindergarten, shifted from presenting *ideal* models (Froebel), to working through practical situations (Dewey), to forming proper habits through stimulus-response training (Thorndike). All these changes produced activities and components of the kindergarten program that can easily be identified in a modern kindergarten, and many of our own practices have their origins in this period.

By 1922, 12 percent of those children eligible to attend kindergarten were doing so (Spodek, 1982), producing a large number of kindergartens around the country.

In the 1920s and 1930s, science began to challenge philosophy as the basis for the kindergarten curriculum. As social scientists acquired the ability to measure human characteristics, and as behaviorist psychology came into its own, the temptation to apply both of these to the kindergarten curriculum was too great to resist. *A Conduct Curriculum for the Kindergarten and First Grade* (Burke, 1923) is a good example of a kindergarten/first-grade curriculum, in which specific classroom activities are based on desired behavioral outcomes, most of which relate to social, rather than cognitive, learning. The creation of intelligence tests, habit inventories, and readiness tests made it possible for kindergarten teachers to base their instruction, and measure their results, on a so-called scientific basis. For example, reading readiness tests measured such things as "auditory discrimination" and the "ability to remember visual forms," skills thought to be prerequisite to reading. It isn't hard to see how these isolated skills eventually became standard items in the kindergarten curriculum, especially when authorities in the reading field such as William S. Gray argued so forcefully that kindergartens should play a major part in preparing children for reading (Gray, 1927). Many thought that the best way to approach readiness for reading was to teach the skills thought to be prerequisite to reading, a practice that is still prevalent today.

Not all kindergartens subscribed to this behaviorist philosophy, however. Gesell's (1925) theory of maturation, which postulated an unfolding of children's mental abilities on a schedule that simply could not be hurried, attracted a number of followers, and kindergartens based on a maturation theory became quite popular and have remained so ever since, thanks in part to the work of Gesell's followers (e.g., Ilg & Ames, 1972). The purpose of a Gesellian kindergarten was to help children "express their instincts" through play, through their senses, through drawing, dramatic play, and listening to literature. Above all, however, and most closely associated with Gesell in more recent history, is the strict proscription against introducing anything (especially formal reading and writing instruction) before the child has matured sufficiently and is *ready* for it. Gesell's influence on educational theory may turn out in the long run to have been marginal, but his influence on the modern kindergarten has been enormous (it is directly responsible for the creation of pre-first programs to give children the "gift of time," an additional year of a kindergarten-like program, in preparation for first grade).

During the twenties, a number of kindergarten programs with philosophies that countered all the prevailing views made themselves felt. Caroline Pratt's "play" school built its curriculum around children's creative expression; Margaret Naumberg founded the Walden school with a curriculum drawn from Freudian psychoanalytic theory; and the Lincoln school at Teachers College promoted musical expression (Weber, 1969).

As kindergartens became more widespread, the question of their relationship to the elementary school could no longer be ignored, especially given the discontinuity between the two. While the days of kindergarten as an educational unit separate from the regular school were numbered, what wasn't settled was whether the largely child-centered kindergarten philosophy would spread upwards or the largely teacher-centered primary school philosophy would spread downwards. In the end both happened, and the debate about the appropriateness of pushing the primary school curriculum downwards or extending the kindergarten philosophy upwards continues unabated today.

As one might expect, the first seventy years of kindergarten education were much more turbulent than the second seventy years, and the period from the 1930s to the 1980s was more peaceful. Kindergartens were assimilated into the public schools, and their curricula gradually became standardized. We would note two significant developments, however. One was the launching by the Soviet Union of Sputnik I in 1957. Its effect on kindergarten was not immediate, but it brought pressure on schools to focus more directly on academic achievement, and if there were any doubt that academics could begin in kindergarten, the humiliation of Sputnik removed it. This led to an acceleration of a process, begun much earlier, of pushing the primary curriculum down into kindergarten. A second development was a renewed interest in the intellectual content of kindergarten (Robison & Spodek, 1965). Robison and Spodek argued that kindergartens had become overly concerned about physical, social, and emotional growth to the detriment of intellectual development. In their book *New Directions in the Kindergarten,* they laid out a content curriculum that describes appropriate activities in Geography, History, Economics, Science, and Math. In many ways this book was ahead of its time, and we suspect that kindergarten educators' strong biases against what they saw as an academic program may well have prevented Robison and Spodek's content curriculum from becoming standard kindergarten practice. Robison and Spodek's complaints about the absence of content in kindergarten are strikingly similar to our own, twenty-five years later. Finally, during this period, the kindergarten became an almost universal phenomenon in American education. By 1977, nearly 80 percent of eligible children attended kindergarten; the figure today is over 90 percent.

By the 1930s, the range of purposes and curricula (in broad terms) of modern kindergartens had been largely defined, in the sense that the major competing philosophies had staked out their claims. But social scientists had not exhausted their inquiries into child development, nor into language and cognitive development, and the period from the mid-1960s up to the present has been especially fruitful in terms of advances in knowledge applicable to kindergarten. Indeed, much of what we know about language and literacy development in the early years has been discovered in the past thirty years. The work of Jean Piaget, Jerome Bruner, and L. Vygotsky contributed fundamentally new insights into how children learn, while the course of child language development began to reveal itself in much better detail (e.g., Brown, 1973; de Villiers & de Villiers, 1979). Children's emerging strategies for understanding written symbols and representing meaning in written form became much better understood (Clay, 1972; Graves, 1983; Holdaway, 1979; Read, 1975, 1986; Schickedanz, 1986), so much so that Clay's term *emergent literacy* is now widely used to define the course of literacy development before formal schooling and the concept of reading readiness is no longer considered valid by a growing number of researchers (Teale & Sulzby, 1986), even though the concept is still widely used in schools as the basis for the kindergarten curriculum. Teale and Sulzby demonstrate that literacy development (which includes reading, writing, listening, and speaking) begins long before formal instruction starts and occurs in real-life settings for real-life purposes ("to get things done"). They also show that children learn written language through active engagement with their world (as opposed to being taught it explicitly). In other words, early literacy is acquired "naturally" (Holdaway, 1979).

Early childhood educators have not wasted time translating these principles into practice, many of which have radically changed the kindergarten curriculum and its pedagogy (Cambourne, 1988; Morrow, 1989; Raines & Canady, 1990; Strickland & Morrow, 1989). One of the most significant developments in the past few years has been the articulation of what is called "developmentally appropriate" education of young children, from birth through age eight, by the National Association for the Education of Young Children (Bredekamp, 1987; Peck, McCaig, & Sapp, 1988). Position papers, reviews of research, joint statements of NAEYC and other professional organizations, such as the National Association of School Boards and the International Reading Association, and curriculum and administrative guides have been published recently, drawing on the views of a large number of prominent early childhood educators. There has never been such a well orchestrated effort to shift both the public's and early childhood professionals' views on the nature and purpose of early childhood education, and this effort has clearly been influenced by the research on emergent literacy (McGill-Franzen, in press). In fact, it could be said that we are now entering a new phase in the theory and practice of kindergarten, as these new findings about emergent literacy begin to find their way into kindergartens across the country.

But as Blenkin & Kelly (1981) point out, early childhood education is not immune to pressures for increased account-ability and measurable results. At the same time as the National Association for the Education of Young Children (the direct descendant of the International Kindergarten Union) was promulgating its developmentally appropriate curriculum for early childhood programs, the Governors' Conference was preparing a national goal that "all children in America will start school ready to learn," and several states had begun the process of articulating the measurable outcomes of each grade level. In England, where the primary grades as a whole—not just kindergarten—have a long tradition of child-centered, progres-sive education, recent events such as the introduction of a National Curriculum have shown that a similar trend is under way in that country. How the pendulum swings!

What does the typical kindergarten look like these days? It is hard to generalize, but from our perspective, kindergartens are still places where children are prepared for first grade. Kindergartners are expected to master a curriculum that assures the first-grade teachers that their incoming students are ready for first-grade instruction: if they fail to master this curriculum, then they need to repeat kindergarten (or be given an extra year in a transition class). The kindergarten curriculum has two com-ponents: behavioral and academic. The goal of the behavioral component is to teach the children to sit still, to listen, to take turns, to fit in with the rest of the group. These are all be-haviors that are needed during seat work in first grade—the teacher cannot conduct her reading groups properly if the rest of the children aren't able to sit quietly at their desks, busy with their assigned worksheets. The goals of the academic component are quite modest and simple—children need to know the names of all the letters of the alphabet and their sounds; they need to be able to recognize their colors; they need to know some basic math (numbers up to fifteen, the five basic shapes, and be able to count to twenty, typically); they need to be able to hold a pencil properly, form the letters, and write their own name; they need to have mastered various readiness skills (for example, understand concepts such as "up" and "down," follow directions, be able to use scissors, have good hand-eye coordination); and they need to

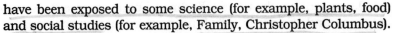

have been exposed to some science (for example, plants, food) and social studies (for example, Family, Christopher Columbus).

A typical public school kindergarten curriculum focuses on a letter or a color each week and organizes many of its activities around these letters or colors, frequently using a commercial program as the framework for instruction. The day is typically organized as follows: first, a *circle* time, in which children gather on the rug and the teacher goes through attendance, the calendar, show-and-tell (related to the letter/color of the week or left open for children to bring in anything they want), and perhaps some music activities. Next, a letter or color or other concept is introduced and explained by the teacher; she also goes through the exercises that children will be later doing on their own. This is followed by seat work, in which children sit at their desks working on their assignments (for example, tracing letters, coloring in dittos, etc.). During this seat work the teacher circulates, working with children individually. This is followed by snack time, which is followed by play time. In play time, children are able to play freely with toys, blocks, sand, and other materials provided by the teacher, or they may go outside and play on the school playground. After play, children gather on the rug for a story and closing activities.

Obviously not all kindergartens in the United States can be characterized in this way, and in fairness, even the most traditional kindergartens are in a state of transition as they begin to incorporate changes in thinking about early childhood education. But this is a slow process, and it is probably true that the majority of kindergartens in this country are more closely associated with a readiness philosophy than they are with an emergent literacy philosophy. If they were not, the National Association for the Education of Young Children would not have mounted such a large effort over the past few years to persuade early childhood educators, including kindergarten teachers, to shift toward a developmentally appropriate curriculum.

Issues in Kindergarten Education

As one studies the history of kindergartens from Froebel to the present, a number of recurring themes emerge. The most fundamental of these is the view of children and their learning. The Puritans in the colonial period held that the child brought nothing to their learning (actually, worse than that, they arrived already depraved), and all that counted (and therefore was to be placed into the child's head) was the body of knowledge revealed by God to man (Blenkin & Kelly, 1981). It would be hard to find a kindergarten teacher these days who would dare suggest that children (as a group) are depraved, but many teachers are firmly convinced that the purpose of kindergarten is to teach children specific things they need to know before they can go on to first grade. For others, however, especially followers of Rousseau's romantic philosophy, the purpose of kindergarten is to provide an environment in which the child himself will come to know, according to his own timetable and in his own way, about the world, about literacy, and about how to act socially.

There are also the related issues of power and of ownership. In the teacher-centered kindergarten, the teacher decides on what is to be taught, the manner in which it is to be presented, and the manner in which children will learn. In a child-centered kindergarten, children control the content and pace of learning. It is significant to us that both Froebel and Montessori so carefully articulated rationales for a child-centered approach, yet both were (rightly, we think) criticized for having such teacher-controlled environments. A careful reading of Dewey's (1938) *Experience and Education* reveals that he, too, was concerned about this issue:

> I have heard of cases in which children are surrounded by objects and materials and then left entirely to themselves, the teacher being loath to suggest even what might be done with the materials lest freedom be infringed upon. Why, then, even supply materials, since they are a source of some suggestion or other? But what is more important is that the suggestion upon which pupils act must in any case come from somewhere. *It is impossible to understand why a suggestion from one who has a larger experience and a wider horizon should not be at least as valid as a suggestion arising from some more or less accidental source.* It is possible of course to abuse the office, and to force the activity of the young into channels which express the teacher's purpose rather than that of the pupils. But the way to avoid this danger is not for the adult to withdraw entirely. (p. 71; italics added)

In the modern kindergarten classroom, this issue is particularly relevant because of the resurgence of interest in child-centered education. Indeed, British infant schools have recently been criticized for the tendency of teachers to simply surround children with materials and do little formal teaching (Maeroff, 1992).

It seems to us that both Dewey and Piaget offer not a compromise between these two extremes but the suggestion that both play a critical role in the development of learning. Piaget rejects both nature and nurture as sole determinants of learning, arguing instead that learning occurs as the result of an interaction between a curious, active organism and the challenge of problems posed in the outside world. Thus, the kindergarten classroom needs to be set up in such a way that children's natural curiosities be given free rein, but at the same time, teachers need to provide a challenging environment in which children's minds will grow. In a sense, both child and teacher need to own the curriculum, not either one, since both are needed for children's intellectual growth. This joint ownership is an important aspect of our kindergarten, and while it is not easy to maintain the balance (teachers carry with them the baggage of needing to control), we have no qualms nor guilt about our active role in the program.

A second issue concerns the content of the curriculum, not who owns it but rather what domains it encompasses. Without being able to spend time in the various kindergartens we have briefly described above, it is hard to know precisely what content areas were covered, but character training (or the more recent term, *socialization*) would probably be the major focus of kindergartens over the past 175 years. Froebel's occupations can be regarded as a form of socialization, as can Montessori's practical life exercises, even Dewey's activities. But there are some common threads running through the early kindergartens, especially if one looks at the activities that eventually become part of the later kindergarten curricula. Nature study that focuses on plants and animals appears regularly, and it seems to have its origins in Froebel's kindergarten. Literature, too, seems to be an important aspect of kindergarten (with the curious exception of Montessori), and the range of literature has broadened considerably over the years (it started with classical literature and stories laden with morals, but eventually shifted toward more realistic and contemporary literature, especially once this kind of literature became widely available). Music and movement (in the form of chants, songs, nursery rhymes, finger plays, and games) has been a constant companion of kindergarten from its earliest days. Art (in the form of painting, drawing, sculpting with clay) also has been a regular feature.

History, geography, and science were clearly an important focus of the kindergarten period in the early years (although one wonders if social studies instruction had more to do with socialization than study of history), and these content areas were especially important to the early progressive educators such as Colonel Parker, William Kilpatrick, and John Dewey (see, e.g., Parker, 1894). In more recent years, as the kindergarten resumed its emphasis on socialization and readiness for reading and writing, attention to science and social studies waned, and only sporadically have educators expressed concerns about the lack of content in the kindergarten curriculum (e.g., Robison & Spodek, 1965). Another reason why content areas have been neglected is that they became victims of the debate between academic and play emphases for kindergarten. The teaching of science and social studies were clearly aligned with an academic curriculum and therefore had no role in a kindergarten devoted to play. It is also true that many of the early attempts to introduce children to science and history were unsuccessful because they either tried to teach topics that were too distant from the children's own experiences or too abstract, or they used materials that young children simply could not access.

Our view is that content plays a critical role in kindergarten, as it does throughout a child's schooling. Curiously enough, some of the early kindergarten educators thought so, too, and Alice Temple's suggestion in 1919 that the curriculum should focus on the three areas of natural objects and phenomena, human beings and human activities, and literature, music, and art makes eminent sense, even over seventy years later. Making content a major focus of the kindergarten curriculum, as the Deweyans did, does not in any way label one's kindergarten *academic.* The critical distinction to make is between a program in which children are *taught* science and history and geography as finished products, using materials and activities that reduce children's learning to mere rote memorization, and one in which children experience science and history and geography through activities in which they can engage and from which they can profit. In advocating the latter approach, we freely acknowledge our debt to John Dewey. The notion that one has to choose sides between a child-centered curriculum in which no attempt is made to enlarge children's knowledge of the world (its history, its physical make-up, its culture, its literature), and a teacher-dominated curriculum in which subjects are taught, seems to us to be a false dilemma. In order to grow intellectually, children, like adults, need the challenge of the external world, and to withhold these challenges for fear they may impede children's intellectual development is to seriously misunderstand the necessary ingredients of intellectual growth. But what will also impede development is simply throwing knowledge at children—telling them science, telling them history—because children need to work through this knowledge on their own: "every new truth to be learned [has] to be rediscovered or at least reconstructed by the student, and not simply imparted to him" (Piaget, 1973, pp. 15–16).

A third issue is the extent to which reading and writing should be the focus of the kindergarten curriculum. This issue is sometimes put starkly as a choice between an academic program that teaches reading and writing skills and a play program that lets children be children until they are ready for formal instruction. At other times, it is stated as a choice between teaching readiness skills and teaching reading and writing themselves. The former rests on Gesell's maturational theory of child development, which has not stood the test of time, and on the artificial distinction between cognitive learning and play. As to the latter, if the development of reading and writing abilities could be neatly bundled into two distinct stages, a readiness stage that comprises the development of the eye muscles, of directionality, of auditory and visual acuity, and so forth, and a reading stage, which comprises actually making sense of text, then this distinction might—barely—make sense. But the course of reading and writing development cannot be bundled into such neat stages, and literacy research over the past twenty-five years has convincingly demonstrated the untenability of two separate stages. *It is now past time to discard the concept of prerequisite readiness skills.* From our perspective, a kindergarten program simply needs to nurture the development of literacy abilities that have begun long before children came to kindergarten, and will continue long after they leave. Some children will arrive in kindergarten with these literacy abilities well advanced, others will enter with very limited abilities. Our goal is to pick them up at their stage of literacy development and promote growth in their literacy abilities as best we can, without stress but with appropriate challenges.

This issue directly relates to the debate about the relationship between the kindergarten and the first-grade curriculum. Why has the first-grade curriculum become a given, forcing the kindergarten program to adjust to it? Why can't the first-grade curriculum adjust to the kindergarten program? The reason is that the traditional elementary curriculum is based on the philosophy that in each grade, teachers will teach—and children will master—specific skills (in reading, writing, and math, primarily). Kindergarten is a comparatively new phenomenon; its curriculum has always been fairly open and unstructured, unlike the curricula of other grade levels. In many schools, kindergarten programs don't even count as part of the elementary curriculum. By and large, the elementary curriculum begins in earnest in first grade—it's certainly the place and time that most children are expected to learn the codes of reading and writing—and anything before then is thought of as preschool. As we described earlier, a constant battle has been fought over the years between those who think that kindergarten should literally be a *pre*school environment (that is, it should be a year of play, without any academic activities) and those who think that it should be part of the elementary curriculum (that is, it should teach children the beginnings of academics such as reading, writing, and math). Increasingly, the trend in kindergarten programs has been, until quite recently, to avoid any direct instruction in reading and writing, concentrating rather on what are termed readiness skills (e.g., letter knowledge, fine motor control).

The assignation of readiness skills to kindergarten and literacy skills to first grade became so pervasive that tests of readiness began to be used to determine if a child was indeed ready for learning to read and write in first grade. Then, tests of readiness for kindergarten began to be used to determine if children were ready for readiness instruction! Once these measures were in place, schools started to hold children back from first grade (and from kindergarten) on the basis that they weren't ready—they needed more time to mature behaviorally or cognitively. The word soon got out to parents that if they sent their child to kindergarten too early, they might run the risk—and the subsequent stigma—of having their child repeat kindergarten. Increasingly, middle-class parents have been holding their children out. If children from a lower socio-economic background are sent to kindergarten anyway, because their parents cannot afford private pre-school, daycare, or staying at home with their child, then the gap between children from these different backgrounds is widened even further.

Over time, what started as seemingly well-intentioned practices by school districts have had far-reaching, and mostly negative, consequences (Shepard & Smith, 1989). They have put parents in a predicament about whether to send their child to kindergarten on schedule, for fear of dismissal or retention. They have forced kindergarten teachers to base their curriculum on what first-grade teachers (we think mistakenly) regard as the prerequisites to the first-grade curriculum. They have increased retention rates to so high a point that schools are compelled to set up separate pre-first grades for children unprepared for first grade. Most importantly, they have perpetuated the philosophy that it is the child's responsibility to adapt to the requirements of the curriculum, not the school's responsibility to adapt the curriculum to the child's developing social and literacy abilities.

The alternative philosophy, embraced by the National Association for the Education of Young Children (NAEYC), and by us, states that the curriculum must be adapted to the developmental needs of children entering kindergarten. In practice, it provides appropriate activities to nurture their social, emotional, cognitive, affective, and physical development. Children are accepted wherever they are in their development and taken as far in that development as they are able to go in the kindergarten year. First-grade teachers are expected to pick them up where they are and take them on in a similar fashion. If it is the case that children's early literacy and numeracy abilities develop over time and at different rates, then we think teachers in the early grades (K–3) should work together as a team to help children acquire these abilities, not artificially assigning readiness for literacy and numeracy to kindergarten, reading and math skills to first grade, and so on. Clearly, what we propose in this book has implications not only for kindergarten but for the nature, scope, and purpose of all the early grades. For example, it makes sense to us to have an ungraded K–3 program. In any event, we think it critical that first grade (and subsequent grades, too) build upon the foundations laid in kindergarten, rather than assuming their curriculum to be fixed and expecting children to be made ready for them.

Except in very rare instances, all children who are legally eligible to start kindergarten should be encouraged to do so, whether they have had nursery school experience or not, whether they are gregarious or loners, whether they are smart or dull, whether they are older or younger, whether they have been read to or not, whether they are well coordinated physically or not. The purpose of kindergarten (as indeed of all education, surely) is growth, not mastery of so-called prerequisite skills.

If growth is the goal, growth in what? The NAEYC (see Peck, McCaig, & Sapp, 1988, p.38) has compiled a statement of goals for kindergarten, based on the work of a number of educators such as Piaget, Elkind, and Katz. The NAEYC goals are:

- Children will grow in their self-esteem, cultural identity, curiosity, independence, and individual strengths.
- Children will continue to develop a love of learning.
- Children will gain increasing control of their large and small muscles.
- Children will engage in interesting, appropriate experiences that integrate their social, emotional, intellectual, and physical development.
- Children will use written and spoken language in concrete, meaningful ways.
- Children will use mathematical concepts and mathematical symbols in concrete, meaningful ways.
- Children will continue to develop control of their own behavior through positive adult guidance.
- Children will become increasingly self-motivated, cooperative, and able to resolve problems among themselves with a minimum of adult direction.

As we thought about what we have been trying to accomplish over the past several years and what the NAEYC sets out as the goals of a developmentally appropriate kindergarten, it seemed to us that our mission could be stated quite succinctly: *To nurture children's cognitive, aesthetic, social/emotional, and physical development.* We define *cognitive development* in terms of children's increasing (1) literacy abilities (reading, writing, speaking, listening); (2) numeracy abilities (math); and (3) understanding of the world (science, history, geography, culture). We define *aesthetic* development in terms of children's increasing interest in, use, appreciation, and understanding of literature, music, art, and drama. We define *social and emotional* development in terms of children's growth in self-esteem, independence, self-motivation, and cooperation. We define *physical* development in terms of children's increasing control of their large and small muscles, and their participation in healthy physical exercise.

In other words, we see the kindergarten curriculum as serving two major and interrelated goals: (1) supporting and nurturing the child's own growing social, emotional, intellectual, and physical development (a child-centered curriculum); (2) introducing children to experiences in literature, science, history, art, and music that we feel are appropriate for children to encounter (a knowledge-based curriculum).

Which brings us to the final issue that arises from our brief review of kindergarten history, namely pedagogy. How do we teach kindergarten? What should be the major instructional activities? There was no such dilemma for the Puritanical teacher in the colonial period: she simply forced a predetermined body of knowledge on children, who were expected, in the main, to study it, remember it, and recite it. There is no dilemma for the teacher who uses a more modern teacher-centered approach, based say on reading readiness, since the instructional activities are clearly laid out in the commercial kindergarten program. Similarly, there is no dilemma for the wholly child-centered teacher (using either Rousseau or Gesell as her guide): she simply provides a supportive environment filled with interesting materials and playthings and lets the children get on with their development through free choice of activities.

Our pedagogy exemplifies both Dewey's and Piaget's notions of education which combines nurturing the child's natural curiosity about learning with the challenges of the external world: it is neither fully child-centered nor fully teacher-centered. Rather, it is based on the premise that growth (in the intellect, in emotions, etc.) occurs as an interaction between what the child brings to learning and what is out there to be experienced. In other words, we are trying to nurture children's cognitive, aesthetic, social/emotional, and physical growth (that's the goal for the children themselves) through developmentally appropriate activities within a supportive environment (that's the pedagogy).

While we agree that the kindergarten curriculum has become dominated by what teachers expect children to master, we think there's a danger in establishing a curriculum that goes too far in the other direction. In our program, we try to combine the two philosophies in this way: we define the general areas in which children will be engaged in various activities, but we design the activities in such a way that (1) children of widely different interests and abilities can participate to the extent they want to and are able, including not participating at all; (2) children have considerable freedom to explore an activity in their own way; and (3) we don't hesitate to challenge, probe, or extend a child's knowledge of a topic when we think the moment is right to do so. Thus, we select the books we read to children partly on the basis of what we think children will enjoy, but we also have an eye toward introducing children to a new author, a new genre, perhaps a new perspective on a topic we have previously explored. When reading a particular book to children, we will let the children participate to the extent they wish, but we will also take opportunities that present themselves to deepen a child's understanding of the book, to reinforce the meaning of a word, to introduce them to an aspect of an author's style, and so on. When we set aside a time for children to read on their own, we don't hesitate to encourage an emerging reader to have a go at reading, or to suggest additional titles to a child who has begun to enjoy being read a particular author.

This leads directly to the question of how we teach the kindergarten curriculum—or, rather, how we structure the environment to help children grow and what we do in this environment. Our approach to teaching has always reflected our belief that children by and large develop their language abilities by engaging in language in a supportive environment. Even before we started teaching kindergarten together, we were drawn to James Moffett's theory of discourse (Moffett, 1967; Moffett & Wagner, 1983), and especially to the work of Holdaway (1979), whose notion of emergent literacy and natural learning made such sense to us. Recently, Cambourne (1988) has refined and developed Holdaway's teaching and learning philosophy, in a book called *The Whole Story: Natural Learning and the Acquisition of Literacy in the Classroom.* As we started to write this book, it dawned on us just how well Cambourne's Model of Learning describes our own teaching philosophy.

Children learn to speak without direct instruction from parents or teachers. What Holdaway and Cambourne have argued is that if we can provide the same conditions for learning to read and write as parents provide children as they learn to speak, we could indeed make the acquisition of reading and writing a quite natural act of learning. Indeed, the act of learning anything, including science, history, and mathematics, need not be artificial. Essentially, Cambourne argues that there are eight conditions that need to be present for natural learning to take place: immersion, demonstration, engagement, expectation, responsibility, approximation, use, and response. We will briefly describe each of these and then give examples of how we establish these conditions in our classroom.

The first condition is *immersion.* Children need to be immersed in texts of all sorts and kinds. Cambourne makes the excellent point that in natural learning, "it is important to appreciate that what does saturate them [i.e., new members of a community], that which is available and in which they are immersed, is always whole, usually meaningful and in a context which makes sense ..." (p. 34). Our children are immersed in oral language and print every day. They are surrounded by meaningful print in the form of books, charts, labels, displays of their work, and learning centers. Further, these displays always relate to themes or topics we are exploring, so they have double meaning—meaning within themselves and meaning related to the themes.

The second condition is *demonstration.* Cambourne describes two kinds of demonstrations—actions and artifacts. Actions typically involve experienced users of the language actually engaging in the language, showing beginners how the language is used. Artifacts involve things—in this context books are particularly relevant: "a book is an artifact. It is also a demonstration of what a book is, what print is and does, how words are spelled and how texts are structured" (p. 34). We model reading, writing, listening, and speaking continuously throughout the day. During the Daily Message we model writing. The children see us composing as well as engaging in the mechanical aspects of writing (see chapter 3). Some of these mechanics include holding a pencil, forming letters, writing left to right and top to bottom, using capitalization and punctuation. When reading big books and charts we demonstrate the reading process. Again, the children see us read from top to bottom and left to right; we demonstrate that print contains meaning and show how we use cueing systems. During our Relax & Read time, the children see us sitting down with a book modeling independent reading (see chapter 3).

We deliberately vary our demonstrations, using different materials. Numerous demonstrations are necessary because not every child is ready to learn from a given demonstration, and some children need repeated demonstrations before they start to catch on.

The third condition is *engagement*—children actually trying out the language themselves. Cambourne makes the point that immersions and demonstrations by themselves don't necessarily lead to learning. We may provide a literate environment filled with interesting and appropriate activities, but if a child doesn't engage in them, learning won't occur. He also says that children aren't likely to engage until (1) they perceive that they can do on their own what has been demonstrated; (2) they see the worth of the activity; and (3) they won't be embarrassed or scorned if they fail in their attempts. An example of a child perceiving that they can do things on their own is Sarah "reading" a book immediately after we have read it to her; and Sean has obviously seen the worth of writing when he writes a note "SAV 4 SEAN" (Save for Sean) and attaches it to a Construx structure he has just built. We know that when a child volunteers to use the pointer and read the daily message, he needn't worry about getting stuck—his classmates are always eager to help and won't embarrass or scorn him in his attempts. Engagement is in part brought about by the fourth condition, *expectation.* Expectations come from within the learner and from outside the learner (especially from those whom the learner trusts): "if those to whom the learner is bonded behave in ways that communicate the message that certain kinds of learning are expected, then that learning usually takes place" (p. 35). The children know we genuinely care about them and for them. We convey this message by being positive, fair, and sensitive to them.

The fifth condition is *responsibility.* Teachers have the

responsibility for supplying an environment rich in print, giving ample demonstrations, and conveying positive expectations. When one of our children is writing and we think it appropriate to nudge, we wouldn't hesitate to encourage him to write more. The children themselves have responsibilities, too, according to Cambourne: for example, they need to take responsibility for deciding which aspects of language they want to engage in after the demonstrations, or which aspects they want to attend to in the language-rich environment.

The sixth condition is *approximation.* We should not expect children to learn all the subcomponents of language before they are permitted to read, to write, to dance, or to sing. Inevitably, children will produce approximations of full-fledged language (in their speech, in their reading, in their writing), sometimes over a long period as they pull all the components together and become skilled users of the language. There should be no fear that these approximations will persist, and they should be encouraged and accepted as a normal part of language development. Experimentation, including what adults call "errors," is normal and essential to language development. In our classroom, when a child is reading to us and making up the story as she goes along, we wouldn't discount her or correct her. We would accept her story as an act of reading.

The seventh condition is *use.* Children "need both time and opportunity to use their immature, developing language skills" (p. 38), both on their own and with others (peers, adults). Language needs to be practiced. Every center or area in our classroom is designed to have children *use* language in some way (listening, speaking, reading, or writing).

The eighth condition is *response.* Responses serve several important functions in language development. They are opportunities for skilled users of the language to receive, and celebrate, the approximations of the beginner; they are opportunities for adults to fill in the missing parts of the child's approximations, so the child sees what the whole looks like; and they provide a framework for further learning. We respond to our children in a variety of ways throughout the day (for example, when we ask a child to say something more about a show-and-tell item; when we celebrate a spontaneous act of reading; when we sit with a child and explain a mathematical process). In summary, our approach to nurturing children's cognitive, aesthetic, social/

emotional, and physical development involves creating an environment in which children of quite a wide range of interests and at different stages of development will engage in a variety of activities to the extent they are willing and able, and from which their growth will be nourished. We make no guarantees that children when they leave us will have mastered a specific curriculum. Nor do we leave the curriculum experiences entirely up to the children, although we would never have children engage in activites that were unsuitable for them. Our approach is not a compromise between teacher-centered and child-centered philosophies, but rather what we call a balanced approach that draws both from the individual child and from the external world, both of which we believe are necessary ingredients for a child's development in these early years of schooling.

2 How Our Program Works: Getting Organized

Why Themes?

Our curriculum is organized around *themes.* A theme is an organizing framework within which to structure learning activities for a period of time. A theme is different from a unit in, say, social studies or science, where children and teachers focus on a particular historical event or character or on a specific topic in science. Themes encompass all aspects of the curriculum; reading, writing, math, art, music and movement, and dramatic play all are brought to bear on a topic. For example, in the theme Animals in Winter, we delve into various aspects of the topic, learning about the preparations that animals make for winter, about changes that animals make in their appearance and feeding habits, and about the various animals that remain versus those that migrate, and we use a variety of language processes such as reading aloud books or articles, having the children make direct observations, drawing and writing about animals, constructing bird feeders from a set of directions, and talking about what they learned. All of our major classroom activities—Music and Movement, Theme Time, Activity Time, and Closing—focus on different aspects of the theme.

Organizing learning around themes is not new; in fact, there's evidence of theme-centered instruction as early as the 1870s. But the concept was popular in the 1960s and 1970s (Smith, 1972; Haggitt, 1975) and is now enjoying another revival (see Baskwill & Whitman, 1986; Gamberg, et al., 1988; Katz & Chard, 1989; Strickland, 1989; Walmsley & Walp, 1990), and it is particularly useful in a kindergarten classroom, for several reasons. First, themes provide a meaningful goal for language activities. Exploration of content becomes the focus of reading, writing, listening, and speaking, not just acquisition and practice in these separate skills. Second, themes provide a way to integrate all aspects of the curriculum. Reading, writing, speaking, listening, math, music, art, and drama can all be focused on the same topic. This makes the curriculum much less fragmented, and it makes the most of limited time periods, especially important to a half-day kindergarten. Third, themes encourage children to explore more deeply into content, by providing sustained activities over the course of a week or two and by looking at a topic from several vantage points. Fourth, themes offer one of the best organizational structures in which children of different interests, language abilities, and background knowledge can profitably work together. In contrast to focusing on skills as topics, where it is difficult to create activities for children with widely differing abilities and interests, focusing on content themes provides a common focus for classroom activities, but it permits children to learn at their own rate, use materials they are comfortable with, and explore aspects of a topic that are of special interest to them. Finally, themes allow us to balance teacher-directed and child-centered activities.

Choosing Themes

We choose themes not only for their appeal to our children's interests, but also on the basis of their potential to enlarge children's knowledge of the world (that is, knowledge of literature, history, science, health, current events, and so on). Consequently, we choose many of our themes from subject areas (literature, science, social studies); we also choose them from the calendar (seasons, holidays, famous people's birthdays) and from authors (focusing on the books and life of a single author or illustrator). Sometimes a theme is developed spontaneously through student interest. In planning the year's themes, we consciously aim for a balance between these sources.

In kindergarten, it's important to create themes that are concrete and relate to the interests and knowledge of young children. What appeals to an adult may not appeal to kindergartners, and vice versa. When we first started creating themes, we were taken aback sometimes at the response to our themes: some that we thought elegant were poorly received by the children, and some we thought rather mundane were great hits. We learned through these experiences what kinds of themes worked best for us, and these are the ones presented in this program.

There are several stages in putting a theme together. It's hard to know which comes first—finding some excellent literature or finding a topic. Some themes have been built around a single book that captured our attention and cried out to have a theme built around it. Other themes stem from the social studies or science curriculum (that is, built from a content-area base). Whichever method we use, once we have a tentative theme, we think about important dimensions of the topic, often laying these out visually in a *web* so we can see what they look like. Even as we do this, however, we are thinking about books we know on the topic, and frequently the books themselves will suggest dimensions of the topic. Sometimes, as we put a theme together, it starts to fall apart because there isn't enough substance to it, or because what we thought were relevant books turn out, on closer examination, not to be as good as we imagined them to be. Occasionally, we find that the theme is too big, and what starts as one theme ends up as two or three (for example, Animals in Winter was split into three themes: Snow and Winter, Animals in Winter, and Penguins). Sometimes a theme needs to be combined with another and presented as one (for example, Pilgrims and Thanksgiving or Bedtime and Bathtime). It's a very fluid process, and it helps to have another person to bounce ideas off, or to lean on when one's own ideas dry up.

At some point, the theme takes sufficient shape for us to decide that it's one we want to use. Once we have made this decision, we gather as many ideas for activities, sources, and materials as we can find relating to the theme. These include:

- nonfiction and fiction books from the school library, public libraries, and our home libraries;
- Big Books, listening tapes, and records with books;
- art ideas (for projects and activities);

- ideas for activities;
- interesting topics for writing;
- songs, fingerplays, movement activities, and poems;
- toys, puzzles, and games; and
- ideas for a dramatic play center.

Next, we look for high-quality literature that will pique the students' interest and enlarge their knowledge of the topic. We also group materials and activities that relate well to one another and can be presented together. It is important to consider the sequence of information at this planning stage: for example, we would want to introduce the concept of a farm before talking about pigs, horses, and cows.

The length of time spent on a theme is determined by the amount and quality of materials we can find, and by the children's interest once we get started. Most *major themes* run from a week to as long as three weeks, but some that we call *mini-themes* may last only a day or two. Animals in Winter is an example of a major theme, and Penguins is an example of a mini-theme (it spins off from Animals in Winter). While Animals in Winter lasts about a week, we devote only one day to Penguins.

We also have *author themes* which are based on the works of a particular author or illustrator. For example, during our Snow and Winter theme, we read *The Snowy Day*, by Ezra Jack Keats. This is a natural springboard to an author theme. We get a photograph of Keats and some interesting facts about him and his work (we get this information from book jackets and from reference books in the school or local public library). Next, we collect as many of his books as we can to place in a classroom center. With Keats, we plan an art activity that provides the children with a variety of materials to make a collage (this mirrors Keats' own illustrative technique). We also read as many of his books as possible, whenever we have some free time during the day. Author themes can be done at any time during the year (sometimes it's fun to do them to coincide with the author's birthday, or perhaps even to coincide with an author visit to the school), and they can easily be run concurrently with another theme. Sometimes the children's interest in a particular book prompts us to create an author theme. Because these author themes don't have formal activities associated with them, we don't set them up as regular themes, but they are nonetheless an important component of the program.

A third kind of theme is what we call a *concurrent theme*. It's called concurrent because it is tucked inside a major or mini-theme and is done at the same time as its host theme. For instance, while we are doing Giants, we also do a concurrent math theme on Measurement. While we do a theme on Valentine's Day, we do a concurrent theme on the Post Office. Concurrent themes may be related to the host theme (for example, Post Office is related to Valentine's Day; Shapes is related to the Sea), or not (for example, doing Magnets during Snow and Winter). We use unrelated concurrent themes when we want to provide children with activities that contrast sharply with what we are doing (sometimes to break up a longer theme), or as an opportunity for exploring a topic that simply cannot wait until the end of a regularly scheduled theme. At the very least, a concurrent theme will consist of a center and some activities. Concurrent themes allow us to explore topics and activities without having to create a formal theme (major or mini), either because it doesn't warrant the expenditure of time or because the topic isn't big enough for a full-fledged theme.

Below is a list of themes we currently use in the program:

September/October/November
Bus
Bears
Sea/Shapes
Lifecycle of the Butterfly
Home and Family
Firefighters
Apples
Skeletons and Bones/Hospitals
Fall and Halloween
Native Americans
Pilgrims and Thanksgiving
Alphabet

December/January/February
Number Books and Counting
Colors
Months of the Year
Nursery Rhymes

Snow and Winter/Magnets
Animals in Winter
Penguins
Martin Luther King
Bedtime and Bathtime
Food and Nutrition
Folk Tales, Fairy Tales
Giants/Measuring
Groundhog Day
Chinese New Year
Abraham Lincoln
Valentine's Day/Post Office
George Washington

March/April/May/June
Dinosaurs
Spring/Money
Babies
Farms
Mother's Day
Plants and Growing
Ecology
Father's Day

Organizing Theme Activities

To organize the teaching of a given theme, we first sort through our collection of ideas, sources, and materials, and then begin laying out the various components of the daily schedule. Although we proceed rather randomly, eventually we have to decide on a Music and Movement activity (a game, chant, or song), a Theme Time read-aloud (either a story or a Big Book, perhaps both), at least two activities for Activity Time (this is the most time-consuming task), and another book for Closing. As we assemble these, we also are looking to weave art and math into some of the activities and to ensure that all the activities work well together to create a cohesive day. We also plan centers. A *center* is an area to display theme-related materials (puzzles, chart of storybook characters, children's paintings, books about the theme). As the theme progresses, we add materials and the children also contribute relevant objects and books to the centers (see "Show-and-Tell," Chapter 3) but we have to set up the centers initially. (Centers are described in more detail later in this chapter.)

Once we started using themes as the basis for teaching, we found that we saw many things in a different way. Some old materials from publishing companies could be recycled for use in certain themes. For example, Scott, Foresman's 1967 charts on *Food, Farm Animals,* and *Story Book Characters* make good reference tools while doing those themes. Around our homes we now find many more things that are relevant to our program: a wooden wall-hanging of a cross section of an apple became part of our Apple Center; items such as nuts and bolts, jars and bottle lids have been used for sorting; from garage sales we have rescued scales for weighing, typewriters, puzzles, records, and so on. Once we start to work on a theme, we are always surprised to find how easy it is to locate appropriate materials.

It may seem from our list of themes that we keep to the same themes all the time. We don't. We add themes or delete them as needs or interests change; themes we use from year to year are always looked at with a view toward improving them. We find it exciting to create new themes, rather than always doing the same themes; in fact, we have far more themes than time to fit them into the school year, or even into this book. Part of the satisfaction we derive from using themes in our teaching comes from discovering new books and songs, and learning along with the children. One of the problems with writing a book such as this is that it freezes existing themes in place, when in reality they grow and change with each passing year and with every new group of kindergartners.

Layout of the Classroom

Floor Plan. The floor plan (Figure 2-1) shows how our classroom is arranged, although the exact layout depends on what we are doing and it does change somewhat during the year.

When setting up our classroom, we make sure that materials are accessible to both us and the children. We try to put them on open shelves and label them clearly. Naturally, we have some long-term storage areas that are not accessible to the children.

The classroom ought to be divided into areas for use in different kinds of activities, although we have found it takes some experimenting to get it just right:

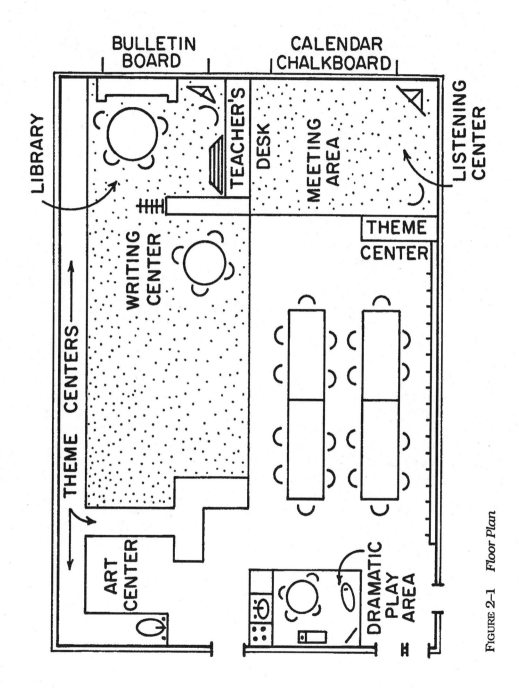

FIGURE 2–1 *Floor Plan*

33

- A large carpeted area for group gatherings, movement, and play (with calendar, easel for big books and morning messages, and chalkboard).
- A library area with attractive and comfortable seating (with book display stands, puppets, and chart stand).
- An art area with a sink (with uncarpeted floor, storage for paints, smocks, and old newspapers).
- A table and chairs area for eating and small-group activities.
- A writing center with table and chairs and a variety of papers and writing utensils.
- A block area, preferably carpeted to cut down on noise.
- A listening area, in a quiet location, with record player and tape machine.
- A dramatic play area, whose materials, size, and purpose can change according to need.
- A storage area for things like books, art materials, and toys not currently in use.
- Areas to display children's work.

Centers. Centers are areas where we display materials related to a given theme, so that children can look at them, play with them, read them, talk about them, even add to them. Centers are created on available tables and countertops, even on the floor. To make a center more appealing, we sometimes use large pieces of cardboard for a backdrop, covered with construction paper trimmed with bordette. Materials are gathered by the teacher, brought in by the children for show and tell, and borrowed from the school and public libraries. Depending on the theme, we tap a variety of additional resources. For a theme on firefighters, we contacted a local fire department to see what materials they could provide us. While preparing a theme on apples, we visited a local orchard and gathered information, samples of different varieties of apples, baskets, and signs. During our theme on animals in winter (Figure 2-2), our center included pictures of how to make a bird feeder, different kinds of bird feeders, books on birds, and pictures of animals that stay, migrate, and hibernate (for sorting). We borrowed animal puppets from the library. A tree branch was suspended over the

FIGURE 2–2   *Animals in winter theme center*

center. Models of blue jays and cardinals were attached to this branch; the children also made their own winter birds and hung them there. Many fiction and nonfiction books were added to the center as the theme progressed.

The current theme is always on a prominent counter; we prefer to locate it near the gathering area. This allows easy access to materials during the theme. When a new theme begins, this center moves to another area of the classroom, where countertops are devoted to previous themes. In this way, children's interest in a theme is sustained for several weeks after a theme is completed.

Classroom Library.   The classroom library is set up in one corner of our room and is partitioned off to separate it from other areas. It is large enough to accommodate at least six chil-

FIGURE 2–3   *Classroom library*

dren comfortably. We use two book shelves, countertops, laundry baskets, and a chart stand to organize reading materials. Books are displayed on shelves that allow children to see their covers (Figure 2-3). The selection of books includes a variety of literature and is changed frequently.

In our library we have a large sofa, donated to our classroom. We also have a small table and chairs and the entire area is carpeted, so the children can also sit on the floor. We have found that it is helpful to organize the books by categories. For instance, the wooden book shelf holds books relating to a current theme (for example, Farm books, Marc Brown books, Animals in Winter books). A smaller cardboard rack with several dividers holds smaller copies of Big Books, *Sunshine* and *Story Box* books, and other predictable literature we have read. The countertops are used to display theme centers, which usually

FIGURE 2–4   *Chart stand to hang poems, chants, and songs*

include many books. Often these books will be stored in a plastic tub or set up attractively to interest the children. There is also counter space set aside for the weekly newspaper (see "Daily Message," Chapter 3). Many of the homemade and commercial Big Books and class collaborative books are stored in plastic laundry baskets. Magazines such as *ZOOBOOKS, Ranger Rick,* and *Your Big Backyard* are kept in a basket where they are readily accessible to the children. A chart stand is used to hang poems, chants, and songs that have been written on chart paper. The charts are laminated to make them more durable. We punch two holes in the top of each chart and attach them to a plastic coat hanger that hangs on the stand (Figure 2-4).

Because a portion of the classroom library is devoted to books related to our themes, this provides a natural turnover and keeps the children interested. One reason we feel our classroom library is so successful is because the children frequently see new books. We don't remove books from the classroom the day we finish a theme but instead shift them—along with the center materials—to another area of the classroom. Consequently, there is an overlap of theme-related books in the room at any given time. We have found that children need this time after a theme has been completed to savor the literature.

The classroom library is a busy place. Many children go here first thing in the day before school begins or during Choice Time. It is also used during Relax and Read as well as during Activity Time. Because the children visit the school library only once a week and borrow one book, we encourage them to borrow books from our classroom library. We provide large manila envelopes in which the children can carry their books. These envelopes are labeled with our name and the classroom number to minimize the chances of losing the books.

Listening area. A listening area is a must in a kindergarten classroom. We've found that the design of the listening area isn't as important as just having one in the room. One year the space we used for a listening area happened to be quite small and would comfortably accommodate only three children. When we wanted more children to use the listening area, we simply moved the record player or tape recorder to a larger space.

One thing we did that makes the listening area more flexible is remove the headphones. This allows more children to listen at one time, and it alleviates the problem of their shouting to one another to be heard. By asking the children to keep the volume low, other groups are not disturbed. Removing the headphones also helps us monitor what is happening in this area (we know what they are listening to and where they are on the tape or record).

Some of the major benefits of the listening area are: (1) it provides a place for children to reread predictable books using tapes and records after we have read them to the class; (2) often children will go to this area to listen to favorite songs and fingerplays; and (3) it provides an area for children to dance and do movement activities that they have learned.

Many of the tapes we use are teacher-made. A shortcut we have found useful is to tape ourselves as we read a story to the class. This tape can be placed in the listening area along with copies of the book for the children to use. The children love listening to themselves on tape, so sometimes we tape them reading a story individually or as a group.

Daily Schedule

The daily schedule for the morning and afternoon classes is as follows:

Morning Class	Afternoon Class	Activity
8:00–8:15 a.m.	11:45–12:00 p.m.	Children filter in, take off coats, choose an activity
8:15–8:30	12:00–12:15	Opening (attendance, jobs, calendar, message, show–and–tell)
8:30–8:40	12:15–12:25	Music and Movement
8:40–8:55	12:25–12:40	Theme Time
8:55–9:05	12:40–12:50	Relax and Read
9:05–9:45	12:50–1:30	Activity Time (start by assembling in large group for directions)
9:45–10:30	1:30–2:05	Choice Time/Snack
10:30–10:45	2:05–2:20	Closing

This schedule gives precise times, but they aren't rigidly adhered to. On any given day, some activities will be shorter or longer. In the beginning of the year, children aren't expected to sit for quite so long, and they need longer transition times between activities. Also Relax and Read may be shorter. In allotting time to various activities, we are sensitive to the children's attention, interest, and mood. (Any time one writes down a schedule it looks very exact, but in reality the schedule is never followed to the minute. We are, by nature, more flexible and spontaneous.)

If we were to have a full-day kindergarten, our schedule would look like this:

Time	Activity
8:00–8:15 a.m.	Children filter in, take off coats, choose an activity
8:15–8:30	Opening (attendance, jobs, calendar, message, show–and–tell)
8:30–8:40	Music and Movement
8:40–8:55	Theme Time
8:55–9:05	Relax and Read
9:05–10:00	Activity Time (start by assembling in large group for directions)
10:00–10:45	Choice Time/Snack
10:45–11:00	Cleanup and Story
11:00–11:30	LUNCH
11:30–12:00 p.m.	Outdoor Play
12:00–12:15	Relax and Read (play quiet music, rub backs)
12:15–1:15	Special (Art, Music, Gym, Computer, Library)
1:15–1:45	Choice Time Activities (continue projects started in a.m.; teacher works with small groups or one-to-one)
1:45–2:00	Story, Author's Chair, Discussions
2:00–2:15	Closing (clean–up, hand out notices, get ready to go home)

Materials

Furniture.   Our room is equipped with the standard kindergarten furniture: tables and chairs, counters, shelves, housekeeping area, blocks, book display rack, a carpeted area, teacher desks, and audiovisual equipment. We have added a rocking chair, sofa, colorful fabric to cover the storage shelves, a chart stand, typewriter, and two homemade easels for big books and charts.

The materials we use for various activities are:

Math.   Unifix and Multilink Cubes, Learning Links, counters (bears, dinos, cats, poker chips), beads, Cuisinaire Rods, pattern blocks, attribute blocks, coins, clocks, jewels, Hands-On cards (from Creative Publications), balances, baby scale, nuts and bolts, picture and traditional dominoes, games and puzzles, measuring tapes, rulers, edibles (fish, crackers, cereals), dice, rubber stamps, and stickers. We also have gathered (from our own homes or from donations from parents and friends) the following items: buttons, keys, acorns, jar lids, bottle tops (from shampoo, detergent, deodorant containers), pennies, corks, bread tabs, coffee stirrers, popsicle sticks, plastic spoons, stones, seashells, tiles, beads from old jewelry, laminated number cards, paper clips, macaroni, and a cash register.

Literature.   We borrow books from the school and local public libraries. We also have acquired a quite sizable permanent collection of trade books. (For a list of these books, see *Teaching Kindergarten: A Theme-Centered Curriculum.*)

Choice Time.   We have a collection of toys and games, including: Legos, Construx, Lincoln Logs, Bristle Blocks, doll house and furniture, table blocks, PlayMobil, plastic/wooden train and tracks, puzzles, Checkers, Old Maid, Bingo, Memory, CandyLand, Lotto, other board and card games, and Discovery Boxes. (A discovery box is simply a recycled lunch box containing materials for an activity. It could be a collection of seashells and a magnifying glass, beads with numbers on them to be strung in order, sequence cards, small plastic jars and bottles with lids to match up.)

Art.   We use the following supplies: paper (construction, drawing, finger paint, etc.), crayons, markers (fat and fine tip), #2 pencils, colored pencils, glue, scissors, brads, Post-it notes, index cards, tape, sentence strips, blank flash cards, staples, paper clips, push pins, steel rings (to make books), tempra paint, finger paint, watercolors, glitter, clay, playdough, and rubber stamps.

Music and Movement. Rhythm instruments, tapes, records, scarves, bean bags, balance beam, and balls.

Science. Reference books, magnets, magnifying glasses, measuring cups and spoons, jugs, water play table, and rice table. Many science materials are found in nature, can be donated, or just acquired through recycling. Depending on the theme, many other science materials are used (for example, the Sea/Shapes theme includes a variety of shells, an aquarium, sand, and pictures of fish).

Communicating with Parents

It's crucial to set up good communication with parents at the outset. For many parents our program is very different than what they remember from their kindergarten days or different than what an older child may have experienced.

On the first day of school, we send home a handbook for parents describing our philosophy and the program. A couple of weeks into the school year we invite the parents to our classroom for an Open House. We give a general overview of the program, explaining the daily schedule, routines, themes, show-and-tell, snack, and so on. After the overview, we show slides of the actual program to give specific examples and bring the philosophy to life. The important thing is to explain why we have chosen to teach this way.

We continue to communicate with parents throughout the year with parent-teacher conferences, telephone calls, and notes. At the beginning of the year, and occasionally during the year, we select one or two of the best, current journal articles related to important aspects of kindergarten and copy them for the parents to take home and read. We also communicate weekly with our parents using the Kindergarten Bulletin (Figure 2-5). In this bulletin, we inform them of upcoming themes, special events, and materials needed, and generally keep them abreast of what their child is learning and doing in school. Thus, they have the option to extend learning at home. If information goes home only after the fact, parents will miss opportunities to help their children expand on topics covered in school.

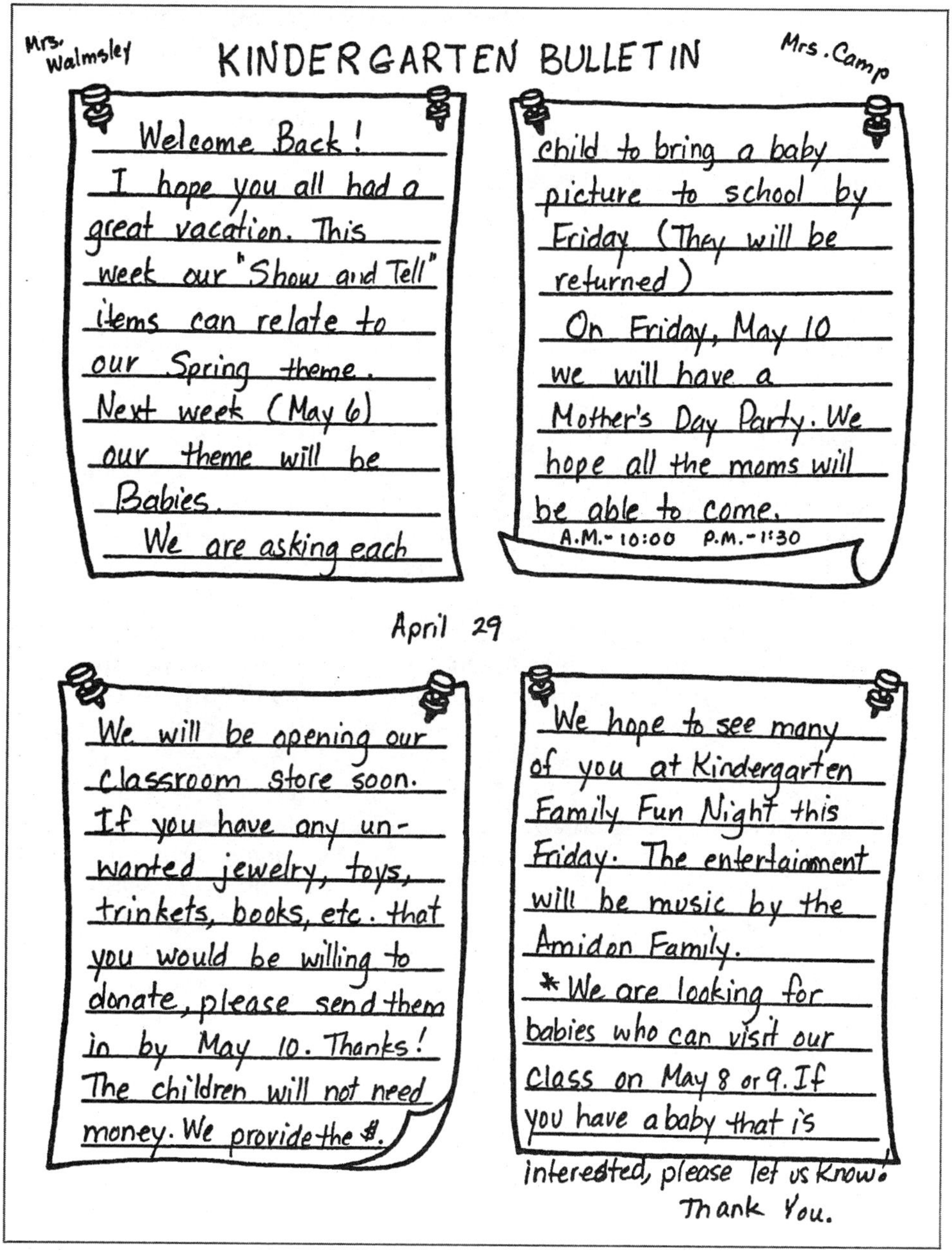

Mrs. Walmsley

KINDERGARTEN BULLETIN

Mrs. Camp

Welcome Back!

I hope you all had a great vacation. This week our "Show and Tell" items can relate to our Spring theme. Next week (May 6) our theme will be Babies.

We are asking each child to bring a baby picture to school by Friday (They will be returned)

On Friday, May 10 we will have a Mother's Day Party. We hope all the moms will be able to come.

A.M.-10:00 P.M.-1:30

April 29

We will be opening our classroom store soon. If you have any unwanted jewelry, toys, trinkets, books, etc. that you would be willing to donate, please send them in by May 10. Thanks! The children will not need money. We provide the $.

We hope to see many of you at Kindergarten Family Fun Night this Friday. The entertainment will be music by the Amidon Family.

* We are looking for babies who can visit our class on May 8 or 9. If you have a baby that is interested, please let us know!

Thank You.

FIGURE 2–5 *Kindergarten Bulletin*

It is clear in the current literature on early childhood education that parental involvement is a very important component of a successful early childhood program. Teachers need to view parents as partners in their child's education. Parents should be welcomed in the classroom, and their contributions, criticisms, and suggestions should be valued.

Using Volunteers

Volunteer involvement is an important part of our program. Because we often divide the children into small heterogeneous groups for Activity Time, it is helpful to have more than one adult in the room. We advertise in our Kindergarten Bulletin for parents, caretakers, grandparents, or any adult who can give their time on a regular basis, usually one hour a week. We have found that it is beneficial to invite all the volunteers to our classroom for an orientation before they participate in the program.

At this meeting we discuss the kinds of activities they will be doing and other matters such as responsibilities, confidentiality, and discipline. We also take time to answer any questions they may have. We want them to understand how important they are to our program and how much we rely on their participation.

Time spent in organizing this support system early in the year makes both our jobs more rewarding and less frustrating. By using volunteers we are able to work with smaller groups of children and do a variety of activities during Activity Time. The ratio of adults to children in the room can be improved considerably by using volunteers. Many of our students come from nursery schools that have two or three adults to fifteen to eighteen children. It is quite an adjustment to come to kindergarten where there may be one adult to twenty-five or more children.

We realize that not all kindergarten teachers are able to get parent volunteers. Other alternatives could be upper elementary children, junior high or high school students considering a career in early childhood education, and community members (senior citizens, for example).

Over the years we have had only a few negative experiences using volunteers in our classroom. For every negative experience we have had hundreds of positive ones. We found that by being well organized, giving the volunteers specific directions, and being considerate to their needs, we have had few problems. Some volunteers are more comfortable with individual children and some do fine with a group, and occasionally we even have volunteers who prefer to do clerical tasks, such as making writing books, cutting and laminating, sorting and filing.

Discipline

We are often asked how we take care of discipline, especially in the rather open environment in which we teach. We have a simple philosophy about children's behavior: if children are actively engaged in developmentally appropriate activities, and if we are sensitive to their varying attention spans, there will be very few behavioral problems. Teachers often misread the signals given off by kindergartners, blaming disruptive behavior on the child, when more likely the problem lies in an inappropriate activity (for example, being asked to sit for long periods).

We notice this especially at the beginning of a year, when we catch ourselves asking too much of the children because we haven't set our clocks back, as it were, to accommodate a new set of kindergartners. We have to remind ourselves to adjust the pace, shorten the activities, and let the children acclimatize themselves to our way of doing things.

At the beginning of the school year, we discuss classroom behavior and make a list of a few classroom rules with the children. The rules usually look something like this:

1. Be kind to others.
2. Walk in school.
3. Stop, look, and listen when the bell rings.

We post these along with pictures to help the children read the rules, and we give reminders when necessary.

Early in the year we also establish the classroom routines and teach the children how to use the various areas of the classroom. We take time to make clear our expectations and why we have them. For example, we tell the children that when they have finished their snack, it's important to clean up the tables so they will be ready for other children. If they've taken out materials and have been using them at the writing center, it's important to put them back where they belong, so other children can find them.

We are both by nature easygoing people, and we tolerate quite a wide range of behaviors in our classroom. Our feeling is that if we are calm, children will be calm (well, as calm as active, impulsive kindergartners can be). Although we can tolerate noise and activity as long as children are productively engaged, we wouldn't expect everyone else to have a similar tolerance—teachers have to decide what's comfortable for themselves.

Every year there are children who test and exceed the limits. When a child does this, we talk quietly with him or her, and to other children if they are involved. We ask them to explain their behavior and make sure they understand why what they did was inappropriate. If such behavior continues, we may ask a child to sit for five minutes in the "thinking" chair, where they can sit quietly and think about what they've done. Before they leave the thinking chair, we talk with the child again to be sure he or she understands what the problem was and how it could be prevented in the future.

If certain behaviors (hitting, pushing, or grabbing toys away from others) persist among the group, we find it helpful to role-play the inappropriate behavior and possible alternatives.

With some groups of children, behavior problems may develop to a point where they disrupt the classroom routines. On these occasions we look to see when and how these problems start, and provide more structure at those times. For example, if we feel that many of the children are not selecting appropriate activities during Choice Time, we will stop Choice Time, gather all the children on the rug, and discuss the problem. For a few days following this, we might structure Choice Time so there will be only three options: playdough, writing center, and table games. As soon as the children settle down into productive play, we provide more options.

For the child who continues to exhibit inappropriate behavior, we begin by contacting the parents. Often they can provide insights that help us understand why the child acts inappropriately. Setting specific limits and goals for the child and regular communication with the parents is essential. Children who have continuing difficulties controlling their behavior need to be treated fairly and consistently, and above all require inordinate patience by the teacher.

Sometimes children's social and emotional needs are such that both they and the classroom teacher require support services from the school or from outside agencies. When a teacher becomes frustrated and is at a loss how to proceed, it's important to seek help from fellow teachers, the principal, school psychologist, and social workers. On rare occasions, we have had children whose needs were so great that we had to have an aide either in the classroom or available on short notice. With such help, these children have participated fully in the program.

It's easy to work with children who are cooperative, cheerful, and follow the rules. Seldom, however, have we had a class that does not have children who test the limits. Children with special needs consume a great deal of our patience and energy, but helping them overcome their difficulties is very rewarding.

3 Daily Routines

We have included the sections on play and dramatization before the opening activities because they occur throughout the day and therefore can be considered as daily routines.

Play

Before children come to school, they have learned about their world through play. We try to capitalize on this natural inclination by providing the time and the materials needed for play.

Opportunities for play are scheduled throughout the day. As children arrive in the classroom, they are free to choose any activity in the room. There are shelves with various building materials (bristle blocks, Lincoln Logs, Legos, Construx, and small table blocks, to name a few). Vehicles, road signs, and a large map of a town are also available. We also have a doll house (with furniture and people), puzzles, card games, board games, flannel board with cutouts, large wooden blocks, and math manipulatives. They can also use the writing center, the listening area, the art area, and the dramatic play area.

Current theme centers also provide many opportunities for play. During the Farm theme, for example, children can play with toy barns, farm animals, and farm machinery. They use the language and knowledge they have learned during Theme Time, Activity Time, and Closing. By providing toys that relate to the theme and time to play with them, we ensure that children are engaged in meaningful play that extends their knowledge of the topics we are studying. By contrast, in a kindergarten classroom where children are required to do cut-and-paste activities with farm animals, they are denied the opportunity to control events and to become involved.

Many of the planned activities during Activity Time provide more opportunities for children to play. When introducing new centers or toys to the classroom, we often use Activity Time to be sure that children know how to use the materials and have the time to do so. For example, when we put out a new board or card game, we take the time to teach the children how to play the game. When we set up a hospital in the dramatic play area, we make sure a knowlegeable person is available to show the children how to use a stethoscope or blood pressure cuff and to keep notes on a chart. This gives the children more information to use in their play, without dictating how they play.

We schedule approximately forty-five minutes a day for Choice Time and Snack Time. This sometimes takes the form of outdoor play but usually children are free to choose their activities in the classroom. During the school year there are many interruptions to the daily routines (school photographs, band concerts, field days), and the schedule must be changed. When this happens, we usually eliminate part of Activity Time rather than Choice Time because we feel children need time daily to be involved in meaningful play.

It's not good enough to simply place toys on the shelves in September and give the children twenty minutes of Choice Time a day. The classroom environment must be carefully organized so there is spontaneity and freedom within a well-defined structure.

The dramatic play area should be changed several times throughout the year. As interest wanes and new themes provide a springboard for dramatic play, the area should be changed. Toys and puzzles should be changed periodically to fit the themes and also to provide increasing challenges to children as they are growing intellectually.

There are many genuine opportunities for reading and writing during play. We capitalize on these opportunities by providing materials that will increase the likelihood that this will happen. In the housekeeping area, for example, we provide paper for shopping lists, phone books, Post-it notes, writing paper,

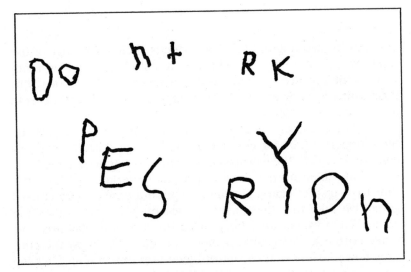

FIGURE 3–1 *"Do Not Wreck"—Ryan*

pencils, pens, and markers. If the dramatic play area were a bank, we would provide real deposit and withdrawal slips, checks, literature about loans, pens, and so on. The writing center is always available if children want to make signs or labels, or if they want to write messages or directions (Figure 3–1).

Many parents, administrators, and teachers think that because children are in school they should be doing "school things." They often see play as something that should be done at home rather than in school. It is our responsibility as teachers to help them understand that young children learn and develop through play. We remind parents, administrators, and fellow teachers of the old adage: "Play is the work of children." One of the lasting contributions of Froebel, the pioneer of kindergarten, is that he demonstrated the value of play in young children's learning and development, and this concept is as valid today as it was during the last century. Kindergarten teachers should not have to apologize for having kindergartners play: it is as essential to the kindergarten program as books are to a reading program.

In describing NAEYC's developmentally appropriate practices Bredekamp (1987) states: "the child's active participation in self-directed play with concrete, real-life experiences continues to be a key to motivated meaningful learning in kindergarten and the early grades" (p. 4).

Dramatization, Dramatic Play

Acting out a story, poem, or song are activities that children enjoy. By dramatizing stories, songs, and poems, children become aware of story structure, characters, and the language of stories. When a group of kindergartners dramatize The Three Bears, they must repeat the sequence and events, know the characters, and internalize the language of the story. Often when a story has been dramatized, children go back to the book with increased enjoyment.

Dramatization can take place many times during the day. It can be spontaneous or a planned follow-up to a story. Few props are necessary. Sometimes a hat or a puppet is all that is needed to stir a child's imagination.

Dramatic play may occur spontaneously, but providing an area for dramatic play makes it a daily activity. Dramatic play allows the children to be in control of events, and it provides real-life situations that are of interest to them. Dramatic play is a natural way to extend learning in the classroom. It provides opportunities for social interaction, language development, and the chance for children to use their knowledge while they play.

In September, we begin with the traditional housekeeping area. We find many children have had a housekeeping area in nursery school and are very comfortable with something familiar. As interest in this area wanes, we transform housekeeping into something else. A restaurant comes complete with a cash register, cups and napkins, rubber food, hats, and order pads. Following the restaurant we might create a hospital with gowns, masks, bandages, X rays, and stethoscope. A variety store that sells miscellaneous items donated by parents and allows children to use real money is another idea for the dramatic play area. A school could be set up in the classroom, where the children could act out the role of teacher, principal, and students. Another area could be a library; children can sign out books, stamp them, explain when they are due back, read them to each other, and set up book displays. A grocery store with empty food boxes, cash register, and money is a good way to complement a Food and Nutrition or Money theme. Themes generally are the springboard for dramatic play. We set up a post office in the Valentine's Day/Post Office theme, and the children can role-play the jobs of postal workers by collecting, sorting, and distributing the mail to classmates. During a theme on Native Americans, an empty refrigerator box could be used for a longhouse. Later, when doing a theme on Pilgrims, the box could be turned over and become the Mayflower.

The possibilities for dramatic play are numerous. Other ideas that might be considered are: travel agency, campsite, bank, day-care center, pizza parlor, theater, book publishing company, hotel, and Disney World.

Opening Activities

Attendance

One of the first routines the children learn in our classroom is taking attendance. We try to capitalize on this routine task by relating it to our theme or asking questions that require thinking. For example, during our Home and Family theme, we may say, "When you see your name card (we make sure the cards have large print and can easily be seen by all) tell me how many people are in your family." Or we might ask, "Tell us the last letter in your name." (These kinds of questions can be used at other times of the day, too, such as during transitions or at dismissal.) As the year progresses, we encourage the children to assume the responsibility for taking attendance. When they enter the classroom each day, the children take off their jackets and go to the attendance board (a magnetic chalkboard). On the floor in front of the board are cards, with small magnets stuck on the backs, one for each child, with his or her name on it. Each child finds their own card and puts it on the attendance board. When we assemble as a group on the rug for opening activities, we can see at a glance who is absent.

We used to call attendance in the traditional manner. As we refined our program we wanted to make attendance a learning experience rather than a clerical task, and we also wanted the children to take more responsibility in the classroom. We were also looking for genuine opportunities for reading. Before long, most of the children can read many of the names. They are not hesitant to remind a child who has begun to play without taking care of his or her attendance card. These cards are available for the rest of the day, and the children often use them in their play.

A number line (0 to 25) is posted under the calendar (Figure 3–2). We sometimes use it for number recognition and addition/subtraction relating to attendance. For example, we might ask, "If there are twenty-five in our class, and three are absent,

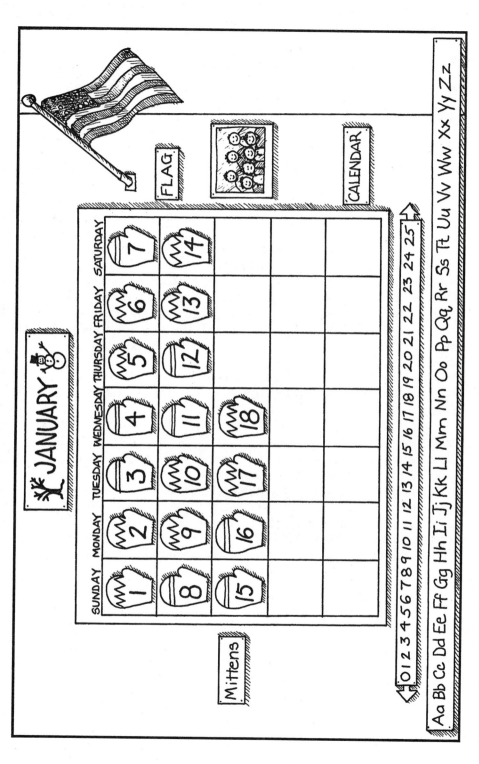

FIGURE 3-2　Calendar with number line

how many are here today?" We point to 25 on the number line and count back three places. It's not long before the children can do it themselves.

Jobs

Another way the children take responsibility for their classroom is by doing jobs. We assign the jobs weekly, two children per job, until each child has had a chance to do all of them. After that the children are free to choose the job they want. Some of the jobs we have found most helpful are: pets, snack, milk, tables, books, leader, attendance, and calendar. If there is a pet in the classroom, two children can be responsible for feeding it and caring for it. Depending on the routine for snack, a helper can get the snack or pass it around. The milk helpers take a basket and go down the hall for the milk. They count out the milk cartons and bring them back. The table helpers wash the table and also assist anytime we need help setting up or clearing tables. The book helpers tidy up the classroom library. The leader helpers lead the class when going to special activities. The attendance helpers deliver the attendance to the office. The calendar helper's job is described in the next section.

Calendar

There's probably not a kindergarten teacher in the country that doesn't do some type of calendar activity. To keep this time from becoming monotonous, we give the children responsibility for this activity and vary it as the year progresses. On the bulletin board next to the rug where we do our opening activities, we have a large calendar. Until January 1, the days of the week are permanent, but the numbers are movable and added each day. The numbers are written on a different shaped cutout each month (for example, September—crayons, November—Pilgrim hats). In January, we do a mini-theme on months of the year, and the children make the calendars for the remainder of the year.

We use the calendar to present math concepts such as patterns. Recognizing patterns is one way a child develops problem-solving abilities. By varying the colors of the cutouts, we are able to create patterns that the children can detect as the month passes. As the year progresses the patterns become more complex.

There are many math concepts that can be taught during

Calendar, including rote counting, one-to-one relationship by using a pointer to count, number recognition, and simple addition, subtraction, prediction, and estimation. We hang a number tape beside the calendar and count the days that we are in school by writing the next number each day. We hang the number tapes on a wall near the Math Center so the children can refer to them at any time during the year.

Calendar is also a language activity. Not only are the children listening and speaking, they are also reading the months of the year, the days of the week, birthdays, holidays, and other happenings that may be noted on the calendar. When a child spells "October" by using a pointer and saying the letters, he and others are learning to recognize letters. When trying to read the days of the week, children are beginning to use initial consonant strategies. The children are also encouraged to put the happenings (birthdays, visitors, chicks hatching, etc.) on the calendar themselves.

The calendar helper is expected to ask the class some questions about the calendar. We model these questions early in the year. When the children take over, they need to know procedures such as how to ask a question (something many kindergartners are not yet able to do), call on a student who is raising her hand, move along to keep the interest of the class, and give some thought to what questions to ask the class. It doesn't take them long to assume this responsibility. Some questions asked by the children are: "How many days in this month?" "Who can spell April with their eyes closed?" "How many days until the chicks hatch?" Sometimes we need to limit the questions because they take their responsibility very seriously! Again, the calendar is not there as a decoration. The children can use this area later in the day, and sometimes we use it for a small-group activity during Activity Time.

Daily Message

As a part of our opening activities, we have found the daily message to be invaluable. The daily message consists of a message, written by us, on a large newsprint pad. The message always relates to what is happening in our classroom that day or to something related to a particular child (birthday, new baby, grandma visiting). We read the message together and talk about what it means and about aspects of its form. For example, we talk about the meanings of words used in the message ("Can anyone tell me what 'binoculars' are?"), and we spend some time talking about letters, words, and punctuation ("Can someone come up and point out all the *A*'s in the message?"). *We find that any skill, strategy, or concept of print that needs to be presented to a kindergartner can be done at this time.*

We model the writing process by writing the message as the children watch. Often the children will name the letters as we write them (sometimes before we have written them!). We read the message as a class so no one is ever singled out or put in an uncomfortable position. Children may come to the easel and use the pointer to read the message after we have read the message as a class. We find that children who can't read yet (in the traditional sense) will also volunteer because the atmosphere is so nonthreatening and supportive. The daily message provides an excellent opportunity to focus on two or three children each day, to observe and assess their concepts of print.

The daily message is left on the easel all day. The morning class writes the message in blue marker and the afternoon class writes in red. Each class reads the message written by the other class before writing their own. Both messages are written on the same page and often include a simple illustration.

In the beginning of the school year the message is short, usually one sentence and quite repetitive. Also, we frequently draw picture clues to help the children read the message. For example:

"We will go to gym." (See Figure 3–3)

Before long, many children will begin to develop a sight vocabulary of words frequently used in the daily messages. Some of the concepts we might bring to their attention when reading this particular message are: the difference between upper and lower case *W*, "go" and "gym" both starting with a *g* but having different sounds, an uppercase letter starts the sentence and a period is at the end. More often than not, the children's questions or comments determine the focus of our attention.

As the year goes on, we write increasingly longer and more complex messages that are matched to the children's increasing abilities to read them:

Today is a rainy day. We will learn a song about robins in the rain. We will examine birds' nests. Do you know what birds make their nests from?

FIGURE 3–3   *A Daily Message written by the teacher*

The children can and do come back to the easel later in the day to read the messages on their own and will often write their own message (Figure 3–4). At the end of the week a cover page is added to the five pages from that week; they are stapled together and put in the classroom library. These become our weekly newspapers and are available for the children to read and reread.

At the end of the year, it is fun to read these messages as a class and remember many of the activities and special events throughout the year. We give each child one of these weekly newspapers to take home at the end of the year.

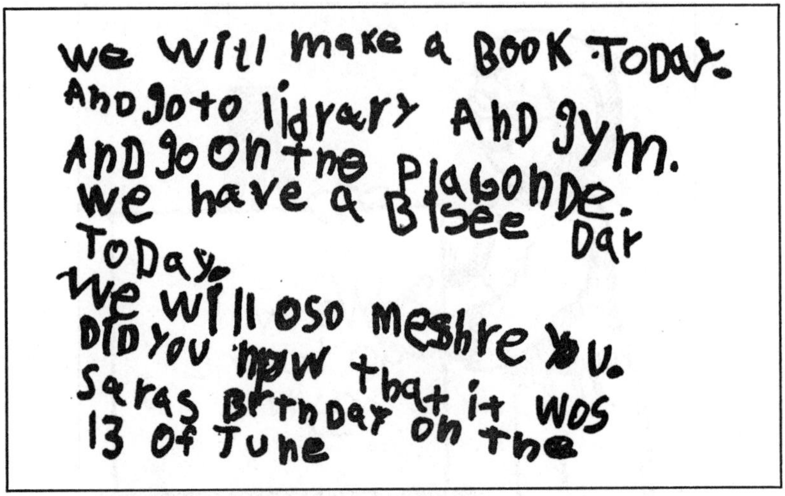

we will make a BOOK TODAY.
AnD goto liyrary AnD gym.
AnD goon the Plagonde.
we have a Blsee Dar
ToDay.
We will oso meshre You.
DID You now that it wos
Saras Brrnday on the
13 of June

FIGURE 3–4   *Children's "Morning Message"*

Show-and-Tell

Show-and-tell has traditionally been a part of kindergarten programs. We have always thought children should have regular opportunities to speak in front of a group and develop their oral language abilities, and we presume show-and-tell was designed to provide these opportunities. However, over the years we became frustrated with show-and-tell because it lacked variety and substance. We felt little thought went into the selection of objects that the children brought to school. It often seemed that children would grab any old toy or trinket on their way out of the door to insure that they had something for show-and-tell. We found that children had little to say about the items they brought in, and what they did say seldom sparked genuine interest or discussion. Let's face it, what can be said about the hundredth Matchbox car, Barbie Doll, or Mutant Ninja Turtle! We would struggle to think of questions that could encourage further discussion.

We felt that show-and-tell could be a valuable learning time but something needed to change. We decided that we would relate it to our theme and give each child one opportunity a week to share on an assigned day. Now, at Open House, early in September, we share our concerns about show-and-tell with the parents. We ask them to help by guiding their child each week in selecting something for show-and-tell. We emphasize that it does not need to be elaborate—it can be something as simple as a picture of fruit, cut from a magazine, when doing a nutrition theme. It could be as unique as the skull and backbone of a cow when learning about bones and skeletons. Sometimes a child may choose to tell about an experience rather than bringing in an object. For example, during the Bedtime and Bathtime theme, children may talk about what they like to do in the bathtub.

To keep the parents and students informed of upcoming themes, we include this information in our Kindergarten Bulletin. Since we began this practice, many parents have told us what a meaningful experience this has been for them and their children. They tell us their children are very enthusiastic about show-and-tell, and learning continues at home. A number of the parents take their children to the public library to look for appropriate books to bring in and share.

The books and objects we receive from show-and-tell in the course of a theme create a valuable resource that we could not provide on our own. Parents and children are very generous in letting us keep the items to use or display in the classroom throughout the theme.

If show-and-tell is not working well, sometimes it's best to eliminate it for a week or two. We have also tried a show-and-tell table, where children simply display their items rather than present them to the class. We ask the children to label the items they place on the show-and-tell table and to include their name so classmates can ask them questions about the items if they wish. Sometimes, instead of having the child stand in front of the group, next to the teacher, we do show-and-tell from wherever the child is sitting, so that he or she is sharing items with the group rather than presenting them. Letting the children ask questions about the item also keeps the listeners interested and involves the audience. With these changes, show-and-tell time is no longer something we must endure; rather it is a time we look forward to each day. The information gained, the genuine opportunities for discussion, and the addition of theme-related materials has exceeded our expectations. We realize, of course, that the quality of items depends largely on the parents' involvement.

Music and Movement

Music and movement is an essential part of our program. It is a rare child indeed that does not love to sing, to chant, to listen to songs and instrumental music, and to dance. While both of us love music, we don't consider ourselves musical, and so it is fortunate that we have access, through records and tapes, to an enormous variety of music for the children to listen to, move to, and participate in. Such is our enthusiasm for music and movement that we asked Mary Alice Amidon, a singer and fellow primary teacher from Vermont, to help us gather traditional and contemporary songs to accompany each theme. Mary Alice has recorded these songs on audiotape and has written out the lyrics and movements to go along with the songs. (These audiotapes and lyrics are sold separately.) With her voice behind us, we have become much more confident about doing music and movement activities, and she has expanded our repertoire enormously

Our music and movement activities have several purposes: one is to give children regular opportunities to express their feelings and emotions through music and movement. Another is to expose them to a rich variety of music, especially the songs, chants, and rhymes that characterize the breadth of American culture. We do this in part by relating the major music and movement activities to the themes, so they are mutually reinforcing. For example, in the Native Americans theme, we teach the children "Return, Return," a traditional Native American song. The activity also helps in changing the pace of a day, and to make transitions from one activity to another. We try to design music and movement activities so that any child, regardless of developmental level, can participate successfully. We have had children who prefer not to participate in some movement activities. When this happens we do not make an issue out of it. They will join in when they feel comfortable.

For music and movement activities, we use the largest open space in the classroom. Usually we write our finger plays, poems, and songs on charts and have the children illustrate them. These charts are displayed in the classroom and are always available to be used independently by the children.

We try to use games and songs that involve all the children. Games like "Duck, Duck, Goose" are popular, but only two children are actively involved at any given time—we wouldn't use this during Music and Movement, but it might be appropriate with a smaller group. Activities like Follow the Leader, Shadow Dancing, and rhythm bands give all children the opportunity to be involved.

The movement part of Music and Movement is not a substitute for vigorous exercise. Outdoor play or time in the gym should be scheduled regularly during the week.

Theme Time

The purpose of Theme Time is to focus on the theme in a large-group activity. Typically, this involves some brief discussion (and we mean brief!) about an aspect of the theme (for example, introducing a new theme, relating one component of the theme to another) and a read-aloud or shared reading of a trade book or Big Book. The books we read aloud come from a variety of genres (fiction, nonfiction, etc.) , but they all relate to the theme. We also encourage children to bring in their own books or magazines that relate to the theme, and we'll read these, too. In our discussions during Theme Time, we welcome the children's questions as well as their comments. We find that if we talk and read about topics that have substance, yet are of interest to children of this age, their questions and comments are both thoughtful and relevant, and they tell us a lot about how they are making sense of the topics we are exploring. There are two kinds of reading we do in Theme Time: read-alouds and shared reading.

Read-Aloud

Before reading we briefly set the scene and provide a link to both the theme and to things the children already know or have experienced. While actually reading, we take advantage of prediction, filling in rhyming words, or we have the children join in on a predictable pattern. After reading a book, we usually take up one or two points or respond to a child's query. But we are careful not to overdo any of these activities because we've found that children quickly lose interest in lengthy postmortems on books they've just heard, and then the activity itself becomes a chore. We take our cue from the children themselves—their reactions will always tell us whether we're doing it right.

Shared Reading

Some of the most enjoyable experiences with books have been early memories of bedtime stories; there's great pleasure in sharing a story with someone else. In shared reading we are trying to replicate many of the positive feelings and benefits of the bedtime story. Big Books have become a standard part of shared reading. Because of their size, there are certain benefits that only a Big Book can provide. When every child can see the print and we are pointing to each word as we read, they see that print is read from left to right and top to bottom and the left page is read before the right page. Children at a variety of reading levels feel successful because they contribute what they can. Because they are reading in unison, no one is afraid to try. The quality of the stories make children want to reread these books on their own; the availability of smaller copies makes this possible.

With the recent emergence of Big Books, many publishers have jumped on the bandwagon. The result is varying quality. When choosing Big Books, there are certain things we look for. The story must appeal to young children—if they do not find the story interesting, the desire to read is not there and their interest is lost before the book is started. The illustrations must be of good quality, add meaning to the story, and captivate the children. The language of the story should be natural—the language children use and hear. (One could contrast this with the language of some basal readers where vocabulary is limited, language is unnatural, and story line often nonexistent.) Finally, the print should be clear and large enough for the children to see.

Certain supportive story structures are present in the Big Books we have used successfully with children. They include repetition, rhyme, and predictability. An interesting vocabulary and characters that appeal to the child's sense of humor are other qualities that help to make a Big Book a hit.

Often shared reading is defined only in terms of Big Books, but we expand this to include other materials to meet the needs of our themes. We make charts of songs, poems, chants, and adaptations of trade books, using large print and children's illustrations.

Many trade books have the potential to be used successfully as a Big Book. Reproducing these in Big Book form or with the children is time consuming but worthwhile. (If the book is currently protected by copyright, permission may first have to be obtained from the author or publisher.) For this, we look for books that have a predictable story structure, natural language, high-quality illustrations, high interest, and rich vocabulary. We are careful not to choose books that have too much text on a page.

Books based on songs also make excellent Big Books. There are many books in which authors and illustrators have taken familiar songs and rhymes and converted them into books. What we do is write out the songs in a Big Book format, have the children illustrate the pages and laminate the completed book. (This, too, may need permission of the author or publisher.) We also put the original songbook out on display for the children to read.

During Theme Time we use many Big Books, but often we will reread poems or songs that have been introduced previously and are written on large chart paper. Whatever we choose, we always consider the quality of the literature and the interests of the children. This is also a good time to follow up a story by acting it out or extending it to puppets or activities that are appropriate for a large group.

Theme Time forms the basis for what occurs in Activity Time. We find early in the school year children may attend for a shorter period of time, but as the year goes on children will be able to sustain their interest for longer periods. The amount of time is not the important factor, it's the quality of the experience that matters. We try to be well prepared for Theme Time, not only in terms of having selected appropriate reading material but also having solid knowledge of the topics we discuss with the children. It's not that we have to know it all—children are constantly asking questions that we don't have answers to—but we know enough to engage the children in thoughtful discussions and to point them to appropriate sources. And we'll work with the children to find the answers to their questions.

Relax and Read

Each day, immediately after Theme Time, we set aside time to relax and read. Relax & Read is simply a block of time each day when children are asked to select books and find a comfortable place to read. We let children read anything in the room—the only requirement is that they settle down with a book. They are free to sit wherever they choose, with whomever they choose, and they can talk to one another provided that it doesn't disturb others. When they are finished with a book, they are free to get up and get another. There's a fair amount of noise and movement, but there's also a lot of reading going on, especially after the routine has been established. We have made a conscious effort to include Relax and Read in our program every day rather than at odd moments, or even at the end of the day. We feel it is time well spent. At the beginning of the year Relax and Read lasts from five to ten minutes, and it gradually lengthens to fifteen or even twenty minutes. We found it is important to make it long enough so that the children have time to get settled. During this time, we sit among the children and read to them or have them read to us. By modeling, we set the tone and provide an example of appropriate behavior. Occasionally, we find some children have a hard time finding a book and settling down. We try to be very positive when this happens. We may need to help a child select a book and actually sit down with him or her.

Like most routines in kindergarten, we find they need some variation to keep the child's interest piqued. For that reason we occasionally vary Relax and Read. We may ask children to read with a partner or in a small group. We may vary the books, charts, and magazines. Sometimes we focus the children's selection by asking them to choose from a variety of books or magazines on a given theme, a certain author, or a series (for example, *Ranger Rick, ZOOBOOKS, Your Big Backyard,* The Wright Group). We have collected duplicate copies of many books through book clubs, and sometimes we ask the children to choose from the Pair Box and read with partners. Other interesting options are playing soothing classical music while they read and using older students, parents, visitors, or anyone who is willing to read to or listen to individuals or small groups read. Perhaps we need to explain here what we consider to be reading in kindergarten. Many children are at a stage where they will only look at pictures and some will make up a story as they look at the pictures. Others will retell a familiar story in their own words. Some memorize a story and then repeat it as they turn the pages. Some point to each word as they read a familiar story, and there are even some that read in the traditional sense. We consider all of these to be acceptable forms of reading in kindergarten and convey that message to the children.

By the way, we don't expect Relax and Read to be quiet! Children at this age vocalize as they read. They need to talk to others about their book and want to share things they find interesting, amusing, or exciting. It is important that they are given the opportunity to do this. This is one way children's language develops—they learn from one another and share the joy of reading.

Although we allow children to read anything they wish in Relax and Read, we've found that books we have just read in Theme Time and those we've read over the past few days are eagerly sought after by the children. They're read over and over, until they, too, are set aside in favor of the newest titles. We can easily tell which books to retain for the theme and which to let go by simply seeing how long they remain as "best-sellers" during Relax and Read. Giving children the opportunity to read a book on their own that has just been shared with the class is an easy way to introduce them to independent reading, and it sets up such positive attitudes towards reading.

Activity Time

The purpose of Activity Time is to provide preplanned, developmentally appropriate activities that relate to our theme and/or provide instruction in some aspect of the curriculum. Some examples of activities are: hands-on math, writing, dramatic play, listening center, science exploration, and art projects.

Activity Time is the only time during the day when the children are divided into small groups. Each day we randomly place children into groups. We simply tap heads or put their attendance cards to one side of the board. The groups are heterogeneous. We choose to work in small groups because it allows us to give individual attention and it provides us with immediate feedback for each child. For example, when the group is measuring with Multilink Cubes, we can easily spot someone who needs help or an additional challenge.

When planning Activity Time, we are careful to select two different types of activities—we wouldn't plan two that primarily involve writing or two that mainly focus on art. Not only do we vary the activities daily, but we also look at all the activities across an entire theme to make sure that we have included activities from all the subject areas and from all aspects of the web. For example, a math activity in the Bedtime and Bathtime theme is adding by counting bears into beds. A writing activity is writing and drawing four things children do before going to bed. A health activity is discussing dental hygiene and learning the song "Brush Your Teeth." An art activity would involve the children painting a picture of themselves in bed or in the tub. In each theme, it may not be possible to include activities from all the subject areas, but these areas are often touched upon at other times of the day. For example, science is incorporated into Choice Time when children use bath toys at the water table to determine if they sink or float.

Each group works at an activity for about fifteen to twenty minutes before moving to the next one. On a given day, we may be working with one group on the rug doing a math activity while a volunteer supervises children making a Winter mural. In the beginning of the year, Activity Time tends to be shorter and the children move from one activity to another as a group. As the children become familiar with the routine and more independent, Activity Time becomes more fluid, with individual children moving between activities as they complete them. At the beginning of the year, we plan Activity Time to familiarize the children with the different areas of the classroom. We also take time to teach them how to use and care for the materials they will be using.

Activity Time is one aspect of the program where it helps to have a volunteer in the room. When assigning an activity to a volunteer, we are sensitive to their own strengths and styles of working with children, and we provide them with specific instructions ahead of time. If volunteers are not available, we ensure that an unsupervised group has a high-interest project that the children can complete successfully on their own. Some examples are: playdough, blocks, puzzles, pattern blocks, and Discovery Boxes.

Occasionally an activity takes more time, and so one activity is sufficient. When there is only one adult in the room and each activity requires the full attention of an adult, we often will choose one of the scheduled activities and replace the second with something the children can do on their own. At times when we become overzealous and try to fit too much into a day, we all feel rushed. The goal is not to cover a certain number of activities but to allow the children to fully engage in the activities and get as much from them as they can.

Choice Time/Snack

This is the time of day when the children can choose from any area of the classroom. Some of these choices would include toys, the theme centers, dramatic play area, the writing area, listening center, library, art center, Discovery Boxes, math manipulatives, or blocks. Often the activities done during Activity Time are selected again by children during Choice Time. In addition to the materials that are already available, we also add water play, sand and rice tables, special toys, and puzzles.

We feel it is important to have Choice Time every day. Because children learn through play, we put a lot of time and effort into structuring the classroom environment. We don't think it sufficient to put out a shelf of toys and expect this to be a worthwhile play experience.

Because many of the toys and materials we provide relate to our themes, the children have a chance to incorporate what they've learned in their play. For example, when learning about firefighters, we provide hats, raincoats, boots, hose and blocks for the children to play as firefighters. When we see and hear children pretending to "vent a roof" or "stop, drop, and roll," we know they have internalized what we have discussed and read about in the theme. We feel that a significant portion of each day should be designated as play, putting the children in full control of events so they have the opportunity to make choices about what to do. And it's important to allot enough time for children to settle into meaningful play.

During Choice Time, we make a conscious effort to observe the children and make anecdotal records. This is an important part of our evaluation.

Children are free to get their snack during Choice Time. One table is set aside for eating snacks. If the table is full, children simply come back when others have finished. Generally, children provide their own snack. Because many young children have allergies, this avoids any problems that might occur if they were served something they are not supposed to eat.

On those occasions when snack is provided for the whole class, it usually relates to a theme or is to celebrate a birthday or holiday. For example, during our Apple Theme we sampled different types of apples; during a Food and Nutrition theme we had fruit and vegetables.

There are many teaching opportunities during Snack Time.

During the Food and Nutrition theme we might ask the children, "Who brought a fruit or a vegetable?" or we might ask them to hold up a nutritious snack if they brought one. While learning about shapes, we might ask the children to look for a square, rectangle, or triangle in their snack. Then we might ask them how they could change that shape into another one.

Closing

After cleaning up from Choice and Snack Time, we close the day with a story that relates to the theme. This is also the time when children can bring their writing to the Author's Chair and share it with the class.

Finally, we give out notices, explain messages, and help the children prepare for the trip home.

Balancing the Kindergarten Curriculum

4

s we stated in the Preface, our goal is to nurture children's cognitive, aesthetic, social/emotional, and physical development. We see these as different facets of essentially a unified notion of development, and in our teaching we do not separate them (actually, we couldn't separate them if we tried). In this chapter, however, for the purposes of clarifying how we balance our curriculum, we will deal with the different areas of the curriculum individually.

Earlier, we defined *cognitive* development in terms of children's growth in their literacy abilities (reading, writing, speaking, listening); growth in their numeracy abilities (math); and growth in their understanding of the world (science, history, geography, culture). (We don't have a separate category for *affect* because we agree with Blenkin and Kelly [1981] that to separate cognitive and affective aspects of learning is "unrealistic in practice and untenable in theory" [p. 78].) We defined *aesthetic* development in terms of children's increasing interest in, use, appreciation, and understanding of literature, music, art, and drama. We defined *social and emotional* development in terms of children's growth in self-esteem, independence, self-motivation, and cooperation. Lastly, we defined *physical* development in terms of children's increasing control of their large and small muscles and their participation in healthy physical exercise.

In this chapter, we explain what kinds of experiences and information we expose children to in the various areas, which together make up a balanced curriculum that we feel best promotes children's growth. This chapter deals with the *what* of the curriculum.

Most of the chapter is devoted to an explanation of the literacy, numeracy, science, and social studies aspects of the curriculum. Social and emotional development does not have a curriculum per se because we feel it unnecessary to focus specifically on this area of growth. All our activities, and the environment in which the program takes place, are aimed at increasing children's self-esteem, their independence, their self-motivation, and their cooperation. In fact, one of the primary means by which we help children toward these goals is to engage them in worthwhile activities that result both in greater knowledge and increased self-esteem. We see no need therefore for separate activities specifically devoted to raising self-esteem, except in the rare case of a youngster with social or emotional difficulties, for which he or she is receiving counseling.

As we have stated earlier, these different areas of the curriculum are separated here, but they are rarely separated in the classroom activities themselves.

Reading

Traditionally, the kindergarten reading program has focused on reading readiness, which is typically defined in terms of a number of attributes a child needs to possess before starting formal reading instruction in first grade. These attributes include:

1. The child demonstrates sufficient language and concept development to begin formal reading instruction.
2. The child demonstrates sufficient visual perceptual development to begin formal reading instruction.
3. The child demonstrates sufficient auditory perceptual development to begin formal reading instruction.
4. The child demonstrates sufficient emotional maturity to begin formal reading instruction.

5. The child demonstrates the understanding of left-to-right directionality as it relates to reading.
6. The child demonstrates mastery of letter names.
7. The child demonstrates mastery of the symbol/sound association of single consonant letters.

As we have discussed earlier, kindergarten is not a time for reading readiness, but rather a time for emergent literacy. Our approach to emergent literacy, including how we incorporate reading activities into our program, is based on the work of Holdaway (1979), Cambourne (1988), and Smith (1988).

Children enter school with a great deal more knowledge about their language than they are generally given credit for. Some of them know the difference between letters and pictures, that print contains messages; many of them have had numerous experiences with books:

> We have come to realize that literacy development does not begin with formal instruction when children enter school. Children bring with them to school many concepts about literacy and certain competencies in oral language, writing and reading.... Research tells us that children learn best in situations that are meaningful and functional. Children have developed their levels of literacy in social and cultural contexts and through interaction with adults and other children. The instruction they receive should reflect to a certain extent the natural and meaningful way in which they have learned what they already know. Problems arise when the developmental, social, and natural environments in which literacy flourishes are exchanged for a systematic presentation of skills that do not reflect a child's stage of development socially, emotionally, physically, or intellectually. (Morrow, 1989, pp. 13–15)

This is why we do not set aside a specific portion of the day for reading instruction. Instead, the teaching of reading is distributed throughout the entire program and happens in several ways. We categorize them into *planned, open-ended,* and *spontaneous* activities.

Planned Reading

In the planned activities, all children are expected to take part. These occur during daily routines. The children are not aware of reading instruction and we don't call it reading time. The activities and routines are integrated throughout the day and into the themes.

The first day of school we take attendance by showing each child a card with their name printed on it. At first we may only draw their attention to the initial letter. In the months that follow, these name cards are used in a variety of ways. For example, during a transition time we might say, "When I hold up your name, go to Relax and Read."

As the year progresses and the children recognize their own name and several others, they become responsible for attendance. They place their name card on the chalkboard when they arrive at school. During the Opening we might say, "All the children who have an *e* in their name can go to the rug for a game; all the children with a *c* in their name can go to the rug," and so on until all the children are on the rug. We sometimes put two names together on the chalkboard and ask these children to be partners and read together in Relax and Read.

During Calendar, the children read the months of the year, days of the week, and other words that are on the calendar. When the calendar helper spells "February" by pointing to each letter, she and the other children are learning letter names. When trying to read the day of the week, some children make observations such as "All the days of the week end in D-A-Y."

The Daily Message is an opportune time to present skills or explain things. As we write the sentence "Did you play in the snow?" the day after a major snowstorm, we might talk about why we put a question mark at the end of the sentence, why an uppercase *D*, how many words are in the sentence, which word starts with the *p* sound, or who has a name that starts like *snow*. Although we spend only a few minutes on the daily message, we have specific goals in mind. However, we wouldn't hesitate to go in a different direction if a child leads us there. Even during a planned activity or routine, we are careful not to be so rigid that we can't respond to the children's interests or needs.

Because all of the opening activities occur while the entire class is gathered on the rug, the tone that we set is critical. Every child should feel comfortable and willing to take a risk. The children's responses help us know what they have learned and how they are thinking. "Learning requires a supportive environment that builds positive feelings about self as well as about literacy activities" (Morrow, 1989, p. 3).

As we progress through the day, Music and Movement also provides opportunities to read. Most of the rhymes and songs are presented on charts for the children to see as we sing or read them. We use a pointer and the children follow along. By seeing the words to a song or poem, the children are encouraged to read them because they are already familiar with them. We might use word cards in a movement game. We might give the children different color word cards and ask them to go on a treasure hunt and bring something of that color to the circle. If there is a situation where a child is not developmentally ready, we would pair that child with someone who is. That way the activity is not threatening: it is successful for both children.

Theme Time is another segment of the day where we do planned reading activities. During Theme Time we read fiction and nonfiction relating to the theme to build the children's literary knowledge base. We expose children to a variety of genres and authors using Big Books and trade books. By reading good literature and having many positive experiences with books, we feel children develop an eagerness to read on their own.

Occasionally during Activity Time we have a planned reading activity. The children may go in small groups with a parent volunteer and "read the room." This means walking about the room reading whatever they can.

Another small-group activity where reading takes place is in the listening center, where we have multiple copies of books with a tape.

At the end of the day we gather on the rug for Closing. We use part of this time to read a story.

Open-Ended Reading

A second category of reading instruction involves more open-ended activities. By *open-ended* we mean that the children are working independently, engaging to the extent they are able. During Relax and Read the children are given time to do just that—relax anywhere in the classroom with a book to read. As we explained earlier, in the section on Relax and Read, reading in kindergarten takes on a variety of forms. The children are in varying stages of emergent literacy. Some will need to be taught how to sit and look at a book; some may have had more experiences with books before kindergarten and already sit and look at the pictures as they tell the story; others will retell a story we have read to them earlier. Occasionally, we have children who read in the traditional manner. We see learning to read as one long continuum. Every child fits somewhere on that continuum, and we accept that as reading.

Other open-ended reading instruction occurs as the children enter the classroom in the beginning of the day or during Choice Time. The classroom environment stimulates the child to want to read. Some of the activities children might choose during Choice Time that foster reading are dramatic play, writing center, charts, labels, games, listening area, and the classroom library.

Spontaneous Reading

Spontaneous reading occurs throughout the day. It is truly spontaneous: it happens whenever a child discovers the meaning of print or makes an observation about print. Reading a label, a sign, a book cover, a name card, or recognizing the same letter in two different words are examples of spontaneous reading. One example that comes to mind is Jacob discovering his own name on a class list of names being sent home for Valentines. Provided the children are in a literate environment, spontaneous reading will occur many times a day.

Sharing Reading

We share our books with the children, and they share with us and each other all during the day. Books are frequently brought in for show-and-tell. During Relax and Read, we read with children in small groups, and they do, too. Often we will pair up two or three children to share a book together. Sometimes after Relax and Read, or during Closing, we encourage one or two children to read their book to the class. When this catches on, it becomes so popular that we have to have a sign-up sheet to ensure that everyone who wants one, gets a turn.

Writing

Writing is an important part of our kindergarten program. Like all other areas of children's development, their writing is at a variety of stages. Some children entering kindergarten may be at

FIGURE 4–1A   *Scribble writing by Jonathan*

the scribbling stage, some just draw pictures, some just write symbols that resemble letters, and others have begun to write random letters (no one-to-one sound/symbol associations present yet). Still others may be writing some initial consonants to represent words. Occasionally children come to school writing sentences using some traditional spelling. (Figures 4–1 A–F)

We know children will arrive at a variety of developmental stages. The important thing is to create an environment that fosters further development. No kindergartner is unable to write—scribbles that are intended to be a letter to grandma are still a form of writing, even though they are at one end of the continuum. Our job is to move children forward from where they are when entering kindergarten. If a child comes to us writing in sentences and using some traditional spelling we expect further growth. Conversely, a child who came to us in September with very little exposure to print and very little knowledge of it may leave us in June writing his name and only a smattering of other letters. We accept that as reasonable progress. While we provide the best possible environment, growth cannot be forced. It occurs only when the child is ready.

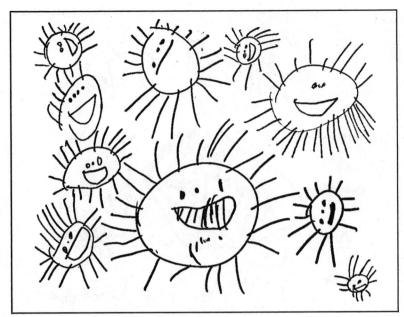

FIGURE 4–1B   *Pictures by Laura*

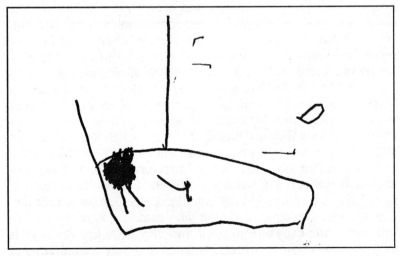

FIGURE 4–1C   *Mock letters by Katharine*

Figure 4–1D   *Random letters by Eliza*

FIGURE 4–1E   *Initial consonants by Erik (These are my friends.)*

FIGURE 4–1F   *Some traditional spelling by Katharine*

We see writing as having two major components—composing and transcribing. Composing is the process of expressing one's thoughts and ideas. When we talk about transcribing we mean the mechanical aspect of writing—holding the pencil, forming the letters, invented spelling, and later the editing process.

Composing and transcribing need to develop equally. One cannot be sacrificed for the other. If a child only dictates stories, they will not learn the mechanics of writing. On the other hand, if a child gets hung up on sounding everything out, this could inhibit the expression of thoughts. We see it as our responsibility to achieve this balance.

There are many times during the day when the children learn about writing, although they are not actually engaged in the writing process. While we read the daily message, they are made aware of the letter names and sounds, capitalization and punctuation, spelling, and other mechanics of writing. While we write the daily message, they learn about composing. When we read a story to the children during Theme Time and during Closing, they are learning the language of books, sentence structure, story structure, and vocabulary. All these attributes are necessary to develop composing and transcribing abilities.

Growth in writing occurs as a result of writing. There are, however, certain characteristics of a classroom that foster this development. Children must feel secure enough to take risks. If a child is concerned about making mistakes, being correct becomes more important to a child than experimenting or trying something new.

A trusting relationship with a teacher is also important. We must have high expectations for each child, yet convey these expectations in a nonthreatening way. Children must know they are liked, and that we have confidence in their ability to succeed.

Children must have a purpose for writing: they must see writing as a useful tool. Because writing is integrated throughout our curriculum, children have many reasons for writing. They are not learning to write because it's Writing Time, as though writing were an end in itself, but because writing is a means to an end.

Children in our classroom are given many opportunities for writing. As with reading, some of these are more structured and take place in a small group with the teacher; some are open-ended. Writing also occurs spontaneously.

Structured Writing

We refer to some writing activities as *structured* because we have planned the activity and each child is expected to take part. Writing books are one example. Writing books are ten pieces of paper stapled together, with a construction paper cover. Each child has his own writing book. In a structured writing-book activity, each child is expected to do something in their writing book, but any kind of writing is acceptable. If a child is only willing or able to draw a picture, that is fine. If a child is writing in full sentences, that is also fine.

While we encourage children to write from personal experiences, we have found that focusing the topic provides a structure, gives them a purpose for writing, and is a natural extension of our theme work.

For example, during a theme on Skeletons/Bones and Hospitals we asked the children to write on that topic. Before writing we read many books, had a human skeleton in our classroom, had many animal bones in our classroom, and had an X-ray technician speak to us and show us X rays. All of these prewriting activities would occur over several days and provide children with knowledge and background on the topic. Children may or may not choose to use this background knowledge in their writing.

Other writing activities that we consider to be structured are books made in conjunction with themes. As we incubated and hatched chicks, each child kept a record of the experience in the form of a small book (Figure 4–2).

There are some techniques we have developed that help the structured writing activities go more smoothly. We work with the smallest number of children we can, especially early in the year. We use a date stamp or mark the date on each piece of work: this is especially helpful when using writing samples for evaluation. After each child has completed some writing, we ask her to tell us what she has written. We then print (with pencil, in traditional spelling) what the child has written. We do this because during the early stages of writing, it is often difficult to know what the child intended to say. By asking them and writing it down, we can see what they brought to the task. This technique proves to be even more useful later when reviewing a child's work that was produced several months earlier. It's impossible to remember what each child has written. When our version of what the child

FIGURE 4–2   *Tara's theme-related record book*

wrote is right there on the paper, we find it much easier to chart the course of their writing development (Figure 4–3).

Open-ended Writing

A second category of writing we call open-ended. In the classroom we have a permanent writing center, where children can find paper and writing utensils. We also include rubber stamps, date stamp, tracers, mail box, message board, Post-it notes, word cards, and writing books. Like everything in kindergarten, we find things need to be changed periodically to maintain interest. By merely changing white paper to pink paper, index cards to greeting cards, interest is renewed.

Children can write messages to the class at this center and post them on the message board, send letters to a friend in the classroom mailbox, write books, or draw a picture. Naturally, all these options aren't provided at the same time. Many activities at the writing center relate to the theme. For instance, rubber stamps of sea animals, farm animals, and insects are useful when doing those themes, and children may choose to label the pictures they have stamped (Figure 4–4).

Another important opportunity for open-ended writing is in the dramatic play center. The centers that we set up provide many genuine opportunities for writing. In the hospital, the doctor or nurse writes medical histories, patient information, and

FIGURE 4–3 *Writing by Kristin with teacher writing*

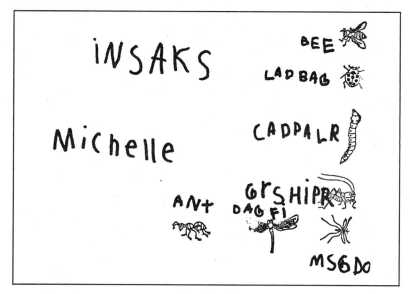

FIGURE 4–4 *Rubber stamps and labels*

FIGURE 4–5 *Michelle's shopping list*

diagnoses on a clipboard provided at the end of the bed. Prescriptions are often written for a speedy recovery. In the housekeeping center, the children make grocery lists, take phone messages, write checks, post notes on the refrigerator, and generally use writing the way we do at home (Figure 4–5).

Other open-ended writing activities include making signs for our room, travel journals, and Beargrams. A travel journal is a blank journal that a child takes on a trip. We ask them to draw and write in them each day they are away (Figure 4–6). A Beargram is like a telegram only made out of a piece of paper

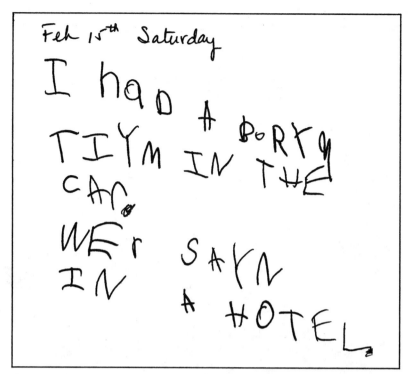

Feb 15th Saturday

I had a porty
tiym in the
car. we r sayn
in a hotel.

FIGURE 4–6   *Brendan's travel journal*

with a Bear sticker. It is used to wish a child happy birthday, say goodbye, or welcome a new baby. All the children in the class sign the Beargram and write a short message if they wish (Figure 4–7).

Spontaneous Writing

A third category of writing is spontaneous writing. Spontaneous writing is just that: a child writes because he needs to at a particular moment for a particular reason. Perhaps he is labeling a show-and-tell item or making a sign for a block or Lego creation.

FIGURE 4–7 *Beargram*

FIGURE 4–8   *Writing to express feelings*

A child may want to give his phone number to a friend. Love notes are wonderful examples of spontaneous writing (Figure 4–8).

Once writing becomes a regular part of the kindergarten program, many possibilities for integrating writing throughout the curriculum begin to reveal themselves.

Sharing

Sharing is an important part of the writing process. We need to provide opportunities for children to share their writing. This can be done in many ways. One is to display children's work in an attractive manner. This gives children the message that we think their work is valuable. Papers can be hung in the classroom, hallway, or throughout the school. Another way to display writing is in a class book. For example, during a theme on animals in winter, each child may draw and write about different animals and what they do in winter. This work can be compiled into a book and placed in the classroom library.

Children can share their writing by reading it to others. The most common way is by reading informally to a friend or an adult in the room. The Author's Chair has also become a familiar fixture in many classrooms. This is simply a special chair the children sit in when they want to read their writing to a group. This could occur informally at any time during the day or as part of the closing activities at the end of the day. While we encourage all children to use the Author's Chair, we never force a child who is reluctant.

We feel the family is the ultimate audience. When we send writing home we hope it is received in a positive way. Because the idea of invented spelling is new to many parents, we explain our writing program in detail early in the year at Open House. We also attach a letter to the first writing sample each child takes home, reiterating what we said at Open House:

Dear Parents:

We will be doing a great deal of writing in Kindergarten to help your child's literacy development. By writing, we mean that your child is putting his/her own thoughts down on paper. This differs from what most of us were brought up to think of as writing, namely good penmanship.

Attached is a copy of your child's writing. Your first reaction might be, "My child can't write!" because you can't read it. However, this writing does have meaning to your child and writing in this "invented" manner helps him/her to develop as a writer.

Please encourage your child to share this writing with you by asking him/her, "Tell me what you wrote" (as opposed to "Read it to me," which he/she probably cannot do). With support and practice, your child's writing abilities will develop.

If you have any questions, please feel free to contact me.

Sincerely,
Bonnie Walmsley/Anne Marie Camp

We have found the most important thing is to be positive. After getting to know the children, their developmental level, personality, and needs, and after gaining experience writing with children, teachers will gradually learn when it is appropriate to accept a piece of writing as is or gently nudge a child forward. This may sound vague to a teacher with very little experience writing with kindergartners, but as teachers, we too need to take risks and learn by doing.

The math concepts we introduce during kindergarten are detailed on the chart that follows.

NUMBER & NUMERATION	
Sorting, Classifying	Sort with concrete objects; explore likenesses and differences, more/less, etc.
Sets	Learn about groups
Equality, Inequality	Extend comparisons; e.g., bigger than, greater then, less than
One-to-one correspondence	Develop the idea that if two sets can be matched, they have the same cardinal number
Counting (Cardinal numbers 1–10)	Explore counting in a variety of ways (number of boys and girls, number of cookies, etc.)
Order	Order sets of objects from smallest to largest, largest to smallest, etc.; develop concepts of first, last; use ordinal number names from *first* through *tenth.*
Numerals	Observe numerals (names for numbers) in the environment; develop ability to read and write numerals from 1–10
Number Line	Use a floor number line for counting forward and backward
OPERATIONS WITH WHOLE NUMBERS	
Combining	Put two simple sets together to produce a new set
Sharing	Share sets of objects (cookies, toys, crayons, etc.)
Sequence	Explore the idea of *one more* through sets of objects
Real-life problems	Investigate numerical problems that arise in school (e.g., attendance)
OPERATIONS WITH FRACTIONS	
Inequality	Discuss such ideas as "A whole is *more than* a half"
Two equal parts of a whole	Explore the fraction concept, using halves
Equal parts of a set	Show that sets can be divided into equal parts

PROBABILITY AND STATISTICS

Classifying information	Sorting and classifying blocks, toys, etc., using two categories at a time (e.g., color, size)
Chance Events	Discuss certainty and uncertainty of events
Estimation	Anticipate outcomes of events
Graphs	Create graphs to display information (e.g., tabulate numbers of birthdays in each month)

MEASUREMENT

Comparisons	Compare length, height, width of objects
Estimation	Estimate sizes (e.g., "As long as..."; "wider than...")
Mass	Weigh objects
Capacity	Use sand, water to measure and compare capacity of containers
Temperature	Compare in general terms (warmer, cooler than)
Time	Use egg timer, etc. to compare duration of activities
Nonstandard use of measurement	Blocks, books, feet, handspans, etc.
Money	Learn the names of bills and coins, in games and play
Shape	Explore and learn geometric shapes of objects in the environment
Counting	Counting related to geometry (number of corners, edges, faces, etc.)
Patterns	Engage in pattern-forming activities with blocks and puzzles

Source: *Mathematics K–6: A Recommended Program for Elementary Schools* (New York State Education Department, 1980).

Math is taught through daily routines, through direct instruction, and within the context of various activities.

Math in the Daily Routines

As we explained in the calendar section of opening activities, many math concepts are presented during this time. Rote counting, one-to-one relationships, number recognition, simple addition, and patterns that help develop a child's problem-solving skills are some of the concepts we cover during this time.

The children are also doing math when we take attendance. We have a number line under the calendar. We talk about the total number of students in our class and then subtract the number absent by counting back to find how many are present on a given day.

There are other activities that promote development in math. The number tape, explained earlier, is used to teach counting and number recognition. When the milk helpers go to get the milk, they need to determine how many they will need and count them into the basket. During Snack Time children often share their food, and this provides practice in dividing sets.

We also teach or practice math in the transitions from one activity to another. For example, we sometimes count the children as they arrive on the rug. We might ask the children to line up in pairs and count by twos as they do so. Before moving to an activity, we might ask each child to show us one way to make six, using fingers from both hands (for example, five on one hand, one on the other; three on each).

Direct Instruction in Math

We use some math concepts as the focus of what we call a concurrent theme (we call them this because they take place along with another theme). Shapes, Money, and Measurement are some of the math themes we have developed. Many math concepts are taught directly: when we want to present a concept or reinforce a skill we use Activity Time because the class is divided into smaller groups. A variety of manipulative materials is used and each child is actively involved. For example, during the Bedtime and Bathtime theme we introduce addition using number sentences. By using beds and bathtubs from dollhouses along with bear counters, the children put the bears in bed. We use cards with basic addition facts written on them, such as 1+2,

2+1, 3+1, 1+3, 2+3. We begin by modeling the activity. We show the card 2+1, put two bears at one end of the doll's bed and one at the other, and ask "How many bears all together?" Because the group is small, we are able to monitor their progress and help those who need it and provide more challenging facts for some. If the children are not developmentally ready for this concept, it would be dropped and pursued at a later date.

Math in the Context of Activities

Dramatic play is a major activity that lends itself to developing math concepts and skills, even though math is not its primary focus. When we set up a grocery store or restaurant, the children price items and count change. When later in the year we set up a variety store in the classroom where children can purchase items to take home, we focus on money. (Early in the year we ask parents to donate old jewelry, toys, books, posters, and other items for the store.) Using a cash register discarded from our school cafeteria, we give children money to purchase items from the store. When given ten cents, a child must decide: "Do I want two items for five cents each, or one item for ten cents?" "If an item costs three cents, how much will I have left over from my ten cents?" The children have to count their money, pay for the items, and check their change. Since the dramatic play area changes frequently, there are many opportunities for including math concepts into the activities in this area without the children ever realizing that they are doing math. By providing children with certain materials and the time to use them, it isn't difficult to nurture children's understanding of math through play (Figure 4–9).

The materials we use are a combination of commercial and homemade. Commercial materials we use include counters, pattern blocks, attribute blocks, pom-poms, Multilink Cubes, Learning Links, Cuisinaire Rods, rubber stamps, and trade books. Homemade materials we've used include laminated number cards that can be traced with fingers or markers and used with playdough. Counting boards (cards with pictures that relate to the themes) are used with a variety of counting materials. For example, in the Farm theme we use barn counting boards with small plastic farm animals for counters (Figure 4–10). In the Bears theme, we use plastic bear counters and a counting board with a picture of a cave. Many cereals, crackers, and cookies are

FIGURE 4–9   *Variety store dramatic play*

FIGURE 4–10   *Farm Theme counting board*

made in interesting shapes, such as dinosaurs, butterflies, bears, ducks, and fish. These edibles often relate to our themes and can be used while teaching math concepts.

Graphing is done as a part of several themes. We graph the buses the children take to and from school, the number of people in our families, favorite colors and dinosaurs, the time we go to bed, and the number of birthdays in each month. On a piece of laminated paper two feet by three feet we make a blank graph. Then we make circles for the children to write their names on. This way, we can use waterbase markers and reuse the graph many times over (Figure 4–11).

Some of our favorite materials are objects collected at home that would otherwise be thrown out. Bottle and jar lids come in a variety of shapes and sizes, colors, and materials. Keys, nuts and bolts, buttons, seashells, beans, and money also make interesting objects for sorting and classifying, counting, adding, and subtracting.

Literature should not be overlooked as an important part of the math program. Counting books and number books are not the only books that can be used to enhance a theme or reinforce a concept. We have found many books that could be helpful in teaching math. Some of them are:

Bang, M. (1987). *Ten, Nine, Eight.* New York: Viking Penguin.

Briggs, R. (1970). *Jim and the Beanstalk.* New York: Coward-McCann.

Carle, E. (1977). *The Grouchy Ladybug.* New York: Harper & Row.

Gibbons, G. (1982). *Tool Book.* New York: Holiday House.

Hoban, T. (1986). *Shapes, Shapes, Shapes.* New York: Greenwillow Books.

Lindbergh, R. (1987). *The Midnight Farm.* New York: Dial Books for Young Readers.

Pragoff, F. (1986). *How Many? From 0 to 20.* New York: Doubleday.

Rees, M. (1988). *Ten in a Bed.* Boston: Little, Brown.

Rockwell, A. (1987). *Bear Child's Book of Hours.* New York: Thomas Y. Crowell.

Wylie, J. (1983). *Learning About Size: A Big Fish Story.* Chicago: Children's Press.

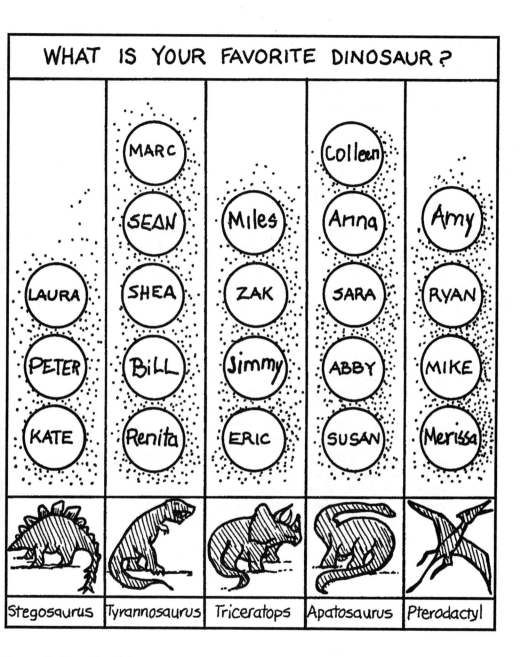

WHAT IS YOUR FAVORITE DINOSAUR?

Stegosaurus	Tyrannosaurus	Triceratops	Apatosaurus	Pterodactyl
	MARC		Colleen	
	SEAN	Miles	Anna	Amy
LAURA	SHEA	ZAK	SARA	RYAN
PETER	BiLL	Jimmy	ABBY	MIKE
KATE	Renita	ERIC	SUSAN	Merissa

FIGURE 4–11   *Graphing*

Rather than teaching math at a specific time using a work-book or worksheets, we prefer to keep the children moving, touching, exploring, and solving problems.

Computers

In our school we have a computer laboratory housing twenty-four computers. Kindergarten students use the lab once every other week for half an hour. There is an aide to help the teacher and students. We agree with the philosophy of our district that kindergartners should become familiar with computers and some software. Many of the programs available for kindergartners use basic math concepts, letter recognition, sound-symbol association, recognition of shapes, and sorting. Basically we feel the purpose of the computer lab is to familiarize the children with the keyboard and the proper use of computers.

Knowledge of the World (Social Studies, Science)

Social Studies

We don't schedule a period for social studies each day. It is integrated throughout the program, in planned themes and in other forms as well. One very important way we bring in social studies is by living together in a classroom, accepting each other and working together. Martin (1990) says: "Perhaps the teacher's greatest role in teaching social studies [in kindergarten] is in establishing a classroom atmosphere where everyone's contributions are valued, where children and teacher learn to listen to each other, and where sympathetic interest in other people underlies all classroom activities" (p. 317).

Children in a classroom will quickly pick up on the teacher's acceptance and caring for all the children regardless of their developmental level, their cultural differences, their personalities, and their socioeconomic status. It doesn't take long before the children start modeling the teacher's attitudes, positive or negative.

As children make the transition from family to the larger social group of the classroom, they need to learn to cooperate and work together in order for the group to function happily and productively; but we also have to respect and nurture children's individual strengths and ways of learning.

We feel children need extensive experiences in social

studies. Traditionally, social studies has begun with kindergartners learning about home and family expanding to include their community, state, country, and eventually the world as children move through the elementary grades. This ever-expanding social studies curriculum is based on the assumption that children should progress from the known to the unknown. We don't adhere to such a rigid progression, and it turns out that current thinking on what is appropriate in elementary social studies programs also challenges the ever-expanding approach:

> The self/family/community/region progression is presumably based on the notion that learning must proceed within the context of the known and familiar and only gradually move out into the larger domains of the unknown and unfamiliar, as the child expands his or her experience. But such a view seems to me a recipe for boredom and sterility, doing poor justice to the expansive capacities of the human mind. Although teaching must obviously take account of where the student is, the whole purpose of education is to enlarge experience by introducing new experiences far beyond where the child starts....Young children are quite capable of, and deeply interested in, widening their horizons to the whole universe of space and time and even far beyond that into the worlds of the imaginary. And all this from kindergarten years or even before! (Philip Phenix, quoted in Crabtree, 1989, p. 35)

We agree with this assessment and with the recommendations of the Bradley Commission on History in Schools (Bradley Commission, 1988), and consequently we explore some topics in greater depth than traditionally has been done in kindergarten. The topics we explore vary from year to year depending on the interests of the children. Social studies themes we've used (and are included in *Teaching Kindergarten: A Theme-Centered Curriculum)* are: Home and Family; Firefighters; Skeletons and Bones/Hospital; Native Americans; Pilgrims and Thanksgiving; Martin Luther King; Chinese New Year; Abraham Lincoln; Valentine's Day/Post Office; and George Washington.

Through social studies, we want children to learn something about the history of our country and about the people who helped to shape it. We also want them to learn about other cultures as well as their own. Our goals are to lay the foundation for further exploration of history and geography and to whet their appetite for learning more about the world they live in and the peoples who inhabit it.

Literature is the backbone of these social studies themes, but we also enhance each theme with artifacts we have collected over the years. For example, during the Native American theme, we bring in real deerskins when we talk about Native American clothing. We bring in shells, birch bark, arrowheads, bead work, and different kinds of feathers. We also provide many opportunities and some props for dramatic play, where children can use the knowledge they have gained. An old refrigerator box makes a good longhouse in the dramatic play center.

Social studies topics may come up in the course of our discussions. We capitalize on the spontaneous comments or observations children make. For example, when David stands up for show-and-tell and says, "My daddy is a garbage man," it's the perfect moment to talk about what a garbage man does, or to talk about the need to recycle and reduce garbage. Children's comments also can be the springboard for exploring current events, but we try to pursue only those events that the children can relate to. Many of the children were concerned about war during the Persian Gulf crisis because they had seen it on the news or had relatives serving in the military. We tried to explain the situation to them in ways that would not deepen their fears but would give them a sense of what was happening and where it was taking place. An oil spill in the ocean, news of garbage piling up in our community, serious storms, the birthday or death of a famous person, the saving of a whale, or the birth of a baby panda in the zoo are a few of the current events we have explored to help children make sense of recent happenings in the world.

Science

A typical kindergarten science curriculum makes few demands and is usually limited to covering such units as Colors, Seasons, and Nutrition. Because children are naturally interested in animals, nature, and a multitude of other science topics, we capitalize on their curiosity and explore many scientific topics. There are several reasons why we think science is important in kindergarten:

1. Children should be learning about their world, expanding their knowledge base.
2. Children should become aware of, and develop an appreciation and respect for nature.
3. Children should be given an opportunity to experiment with and explore science-related materials.

Many of our themes are directly related to science; Sea/Shapes, Life Cycle of the Butterfly, Bears, Apples, Skeletons and Bones, Fall and Halloween, Colors, Snow and Winter, Food and Nutrition, Animals in Winter, Penguins, Magnets, Dinosaurs, Plants and Growing, Spring, Farms, and Ecology. During these themes, we do many projects during Activity Time directly related to science, and encourage children to pursue them on their own during Choice Time.

We also integrate science into many other themes. For example, during our Native American theme, we read about corn and learn that the Indians made popcorn. As part of this theme, we pop corn and talk about why the kernels pop. When talking about bath toys in our Bedtime and Bathtime theme, we experiment with the bath toys to determine which sink and which float, and why they do so.

Many of the activities provided during Choice Time encourage children to experiment with and explore scientific principles. Water play is one of them. When the water table is first set up in the classroom, we provide the children with devices for measuring, pouring, and squirting and ample time for them to experiment. After a while, we take it a step further by suggesting tasks for the children. We write the tasks on chart paper and place the chart stand near the water table (Figure 4–12).

These provide a focus for the children's water play and experimentation and assures us that they are going beyond simple play. We are also exposing children to the language of science. We always draw pictures to accompany the text in these charts, so that after we have read the tasks aloud, the children can return to them later and still understand them.

Later, to extend this exploration further, we ask the children to record their findings. One way we do this is to give the children a piece of paper and ask them to record three items that float and three items that sink. They can draw their responses or write them—often, they do both.

FIGURE 4–12   *Tasks for Water Play during Choice Time*

Another activity we set up in January is the rice table. We follow a pattern similar to the water table. At other times of the year, we do similar things with magnets, sand play, and bubbles.

A classroom pet is an ideal way to teach children how to care for living things. It doesn't matter what pet is chosen. The important thing is to include the children in the care, feeding, and handling of the pet. The needs and proper handling of pets will need to be explained to kindergartners, and even this provides a genuine opportunity for reading (finding out the needs of a specific pet), writing (signs for the cage or aquarium), discussion, and using resources outside the classroom (for example, having a vet come into the classroom to explain how a pet rabbit should be treated; making a class visit to a pet store to select a new pet). The pet center will become a very popular area in the classroom.

We have found the teacher's scientific interest and knowledge to be critical in the success of a kindergarten science curriculum. Children are naturally curious about science, and they need to be challenged in this area by a teacher who is curious, interested, and willing to take the time to become informed about science, even if that isn't his or her natural inclination.

Books, pictures from magazines such as *Your Big Backyard*, games, and objects and artifacts make up the bulk of our science materials. Much of what we use to teach science is either gathered from nature or found in the home: milk cartons are reused to make bird feeders for the Animals in Winter theme; dishpans, measuring cups, turkey basters, funnels, and straws are used for water play. We also use things found in nature: seashells, caterpillars, chrysalises, butterflies, pine cones, apples, bones, and leaves to name a few.

Aesthetic Development

Literature
Literature is the major component of all our themes. A good book is often the inspiration for a theme itself. We frequently determine the length of a theme by the number of good books available.

There are certain qualities we look for in books we read to the children:

1. The story is well written and appealing to children.
2. The illustrations are of high quality and add meaning to the story.
3. The book contributes to the theme, either providing important information (such as *Egg to Chick* by M.E. Selsam) or telling a good story (such as *The Chick and the Duckling* by M. Ginsburg).

What counts as a good book depends on what we are trying to accomplish. Some nonfiction books we have used are not colorful or visually appealing, but we know the content is valuable and is presented in a way that is interesting to the children. We have found that authors who tell a story as they present facts tend to capture a kindergartner's interest better than those that just present facts.

We feel it is important to have a balance of nonfiction and fiction. Although the majority of books for kindergartners are fiction, increasingly there are more fine quality nonfiction books on the market appropriate for kindergartners. When the photographs and illustrations are outstanding but the text is too lengthy, we simply read a portion of the text or just explain the pictures.

Poetry is an often underrated component of a kindergarten program. The language of poetry and rhyming are both important reasons for exposing children to poetry. We have had no difficulty finding good collections that include poems that relate well to our themes.

Kindergartners should be exposed to a variety of genres (see Huck, Hepler & Hickman, 1987): nursery rhymes, folk tales, fairy tales, poetry, biography, historical fiction, fantasy, and books based on songs. It's also important to introduce kindergartners to a variety of authors and illustrators and discuss their styles. We often create an area in the classroom library devoted to an author or illustrator.

Art

Art is one way for children to respond to literature, develop themes, and express themselves. We set aside one area of the classroom to use and store art materials. These are available to the children during Activity Time and during Choice Time. We use a variety of media while doing projects that relate to themes: playdough, clay, watercolors, tempera, finger paints, pottery clay, crayons, chalk, felt markers, and fabric crayons. When using a new medium we take the time to show the children how to use it and care for it. Generally we do open-ended activities. If a project is too structured and all the products are expected to look the same, some children will not succeed and become frustrated. With more open-ended projects the message is one of acceptance, encouraging the children to be more creative.

There are so many ways to expand and enhance a theme

through art. A mural of prehistoric life gives the children a chance to show what they have learned about dinosaurs. During a theme on apples, each child paints an orchard scene. Although we select the topic and the materials, each finished product is the child's, and no two are alike.

Another art project that is available to the children is what we call the Invention Box. We collect scraps, empty boxes, toilet paper tubes, sequins, cardboard, and any recyclable junk we can lay our hands on. We select a variety of things from our collection of junk and put it into the Invention Box. The children are free to use these materials in any way they like.

Many kindergarten teachers shy away from providing art experiences because they don't consider themselves to be artistic or creative. In our judgment, the teacher's own artistic ability is not that important. Providing the time and materials for children to experiment and explore without adult interference is what's important. The process not the product is what matters at this age. The best way to assure that this will happen is by simply providing a table, shelf, or cart where a variety of art materials and paper are clearly labeled and available to children and then encouraging them to explore across a variety of media.

Music and Movement

We feel that children should be successful in music and movement activities regardless of their developmental level. The NAEYC's description of developmentally appropriate practices recommends that "children have daily opportunities for aesthetic expression and appreciation through art and music" and that "they experiment [with] and enjoy various forms of music.... Art, music, movement... are integrated throughout each day as relevant to the curriculum and as needed for children to express themselves aesthetically and physically and to express ideas and feelings" (Bredekamp, 1987, pp. 56, 72). Among our purposes for including music in the program are:

1. Music and movement is a source of enjoyment.
2. Music and movement can be a useful teaching tool.
3. Children can express their feelings and emotions through music and movement.
4. Learning and singing songs increases vocabulary knowledge, develops memory and language, and the ability to follow directions.

5. Music and movement helps develop a sense of rhythm.
6. Music and movement can help to change the mood of a classroom.
7. Music and movement promotes social interaction.
8. Children need to be exposed to a variety of musical genres and a variety of movement activities, such as games and chants.
9. Music and movement helps develop coordination.

Because our children do not go to a special music teacher at school, we feel it is our responsibility to provide music in our program. Indeed, each one of the themes has related music and movement activities, much of it specially designed for particular themes. The Music and Movement portion of the day can easily be carried out with little musical knowledge or talent when using the tapes provided in the *Teaching Kindergarten: A Theme-Centered Curriculum.*

In addition to the Music and Movement segment of the day, we integrate music into other parts of the day. A number of the commercial tapes that accompany Big Books are excellent sources of music experiences combined with language arts. We also use songs to facilitate transitions between activities or to call children to the rug. During Relax and Read we often play soothing classical music to create a restful atmosphere. During Choice Time/Snack we occasionally play holiday, instrumental, or popular music. Each year we invite the school's music teacher to bring his instruments to the classroom so the children have the opportunity to see and hear the instruments and to ask questions about them.

When we reflect on our own experiences in music over the years, we have very pleasant memories. By providing our children with varied and sustained musical experiences, we hope to whet their appetites for future experiences with music.

Most of the songs we choose to accompany themes lend themselves to movement activities. Children are encouraged to dramatize songs and express themselves through movement as they sing or listen to music. When we sing about a snowman melting, children slowly melt themselves away. During the theme on Food and Nutrition, children pretend to make peanut butter and jam sandwiches while they sing and dance to the song "Peanut Butter."

Physical Education

In a half-day kindergarten, there is little time for a formal physical education program. Our children meet with the physical education teacher for about fifteen minutes a week. During good weather we go outdoors and play games and use the playground equipment. If we were teaching a full-day program, we would go outside daily and expand the physical education program.

Although the children move around and get some exercise through the daily Music and Movement activities, we don't consider these an adequate substitute for daily, vigorous exercise, as recommended in exercise and fitness guidelines for elementary children (see Greene & Adeyanju, 1991). As a consequence, we strongly encourage parents to assume a major responsibility for their children's physical exercise, and we offer them the following suggestions:

1. Have children regularly play outside (in a backyard, in a local playground).
2. Have children join a YMCA or similar organization (for example, a local softball or soccer club), and participate in swimming and other recreational sports.
3. Take walks and/or bicycle rides with children.

Summary

In summary, our curriculum is primarily made up of activities that nurture children's development of literacy and numeracy, aesthetics, and knowledge of the world. We also try to help them develop physically, socially, and emotionally.

As we reflect on how much we try to pack into a scant two and a half hours a day, it seems rather daunting. But in practice it isn't, and teachers shouldn't be put off by what seems to be a challenging kindergarten curriculum.

What's important to bear in mind is that one area shouldn't be emphasized at the expense of others—they are all important aspects of a child's growth, It's tempting, given the current interest in emergent literacy, to spend a disproportional amount of time immersing children in literature and composing. But this isn't healthy if as a consequence science, history, music and movement, art, drama, or play are neglected.

We have found that by carefully weaving the content areas into the activities that make up the themes, we don't find ourselves overdoing one area at the expense of another. Also, by integrating the various areas into related activities (for example, combining the study of history with reading, writing, music, and art), we are able to cover a great deal more than we would by treating them as separate areas of study. Most of the time, the children are not aware that we have a curriculum; they see it as series of interesting activities that engage them in listening, reading, writing, playing, music and movement, and drama.

Finally, it's important to remember that the goal is to nurture children's intellectual, social and emotional, aesthetic, and physical growth, not to simply cover a curriculum. Thus, the major focus of our curriculum planning is ensuring that we create and balance activities that contribute to these various facets of their development. (The specifics of this curriculum are presented in *Teaching Kindergarten: A Theme-Centered Curriculum.*)

Evaluation 5

At the outset, we should point out that although this chapter is about evaluation and is separated from the chapters on instruction, we don't consider evaluation to be separate from instruction, and are quite uncomfortable even thinking about it apart from the daily learning activities. But we felt that it would have been unnecessarily complicated to have woven this topic into the preceding chapters.

In the traditional kindergarten program, children are usually evaluated before they enter school and again at the end of the year. The purpose of the former is sometimes to check for giftedness or handicapping conditions (mandated in New York state where we teach), but mostly to see if children have mastered what are called prerequisite or readiness skills and are ready for kindergarten; the latter evaluation is to determine whether they have mastered reading readiness and social skills and are ready for first grade. In our approach, which has no entry or exit conditions and no fixed curriculum, these pre- and post-screens are unnecessary, other than to meet the requirement for screening for giftedness and handicapping conditions. More importantly, our view of evaluation is that it serves an ongoing purpose of letting us know how children are progressing throughout the year; it is not a twice-a-year exercise to place a child on a continuum of readiness skills.

In the first few days of kindergarten, we meet with our

students and their parents, in groups of four of five, for about an hour. During these meetings, we read a story to the children, ask them to draw a picture and write their name, watch them play with other children, and teach them a song. While the children are playing, we spend some time with individual children and talk to their parents. These meetings allow us to gather some basic information about each child's development; they also help the children to familiarize themselves with the classroom and their classmates. This is the beginning of our evaluation process.

We use this information partly to meet the state's mandate to screen for giftedness or handicapping conditions, but mostly as a guide to providing activities appropriate to the range of children's stages of development. We accept children with whatever skills and knowledge they bring with them, but it's helpful to know something about what they bring with them, so we can plan accordingly.

An overriding consideration we bear in mind while we are observing and describing each child's progress is to relate our assessment back to our goals for the program. All too frequently, teachers become caught up in elaborate schemes for assessing children's progress and forget what it was they were aiming for in the first place. As we think about how our children are doing in the program, we focus on our goals, summed up by the single statement of our purpose: *To nurture children's cognitive, aesthetic, social/emotional, and physical development, through developmentally appropriate activities within a supportive environment.*

As we have said earlier, these different areas of development are not independent of one another, and our program seeks to nurture children's growth in all of them simultaneously without making artificial distinctions between them. But we have found it helpful, for the purposes of planning the program, and now in this chapter on assessing children's growth, to consider them one at a time. We only separate them to make it easier for us to ensure that they are given proper attention in both the design and the evaluation of the program. At all other times, we consider them to be inseparable aspects of the child's development.

It will be seen that there are two emphases in our mission—one is to nurture children's growth, the other is to do this through developmentally appropriate activities in a supportive environment. Thus, there are two emphases in our evaluation, one that focuses on the nature and extent of a child's growth, the other that focuses on the appropriateness of the activities and the supportiveness of the environment. These form the categories within which we observe children's progress.

It seems to us that there are three related but distinguishable purposes for evaluation:

1. We need to know where individual children are in their development (of literacy, of math concepts, of scientific and social studies knowledge) so we can provide appropriate experiences, responses, and assistance (this is formative evaluation).
2. We need information about our children's growing competence in language and other areas so we can describe and explain this growth to parents, to our school district, and to our colleagues who will be teaching our children next year (this is summative evaluation).
3. We need information about how well the program as a whole meets the needs of children, their parents, and our school (this is program evaluation).

Formative Evaluation

We need to know where our children are in their development, and we need this information on a daily basis, not just before or after the program. We evaluate children's progress in different areas by gathering information as children engage in the various activities throughout the day.

To observe children's progress in literacy, we use observations, anecdotal records, and samples of work. We gather this information during Opening (attendance and morning message), Theme Time, Relax and Read, in some of the activities during Activity Time, during Choice Time, and in Closing.

To evaluate progress in math, we observe and make records of children's performance during Opening (calendar, attendance, and daily message), some of the activities during Activity Time, and during Choice Time.

To evaluate progress in science and social studies, we use observations, anecdotal records, and samples of children's work.

The technique we use most is *observing children in their daily activities, and recording these observations either mentally or on paper.* Periodically, these observations are transferred onto anecdotal records we keep on each child, and these are used to help us complete a checklist of the milestones children pass and the attributes they demonstrate. This is not an exact science, and like many others in the field (e.g., Cambourne & Turbill, 1990; Goodman, Goodman & Hood, 1989; Morrow & Smith, 1990; Tierney, Carter, & Desai, 1991), we are still feeling our way toward appropriate and manageable techniques for describing and assessing children's growing competence in skills and knowledge.

Since the children are presented with daily opportunities to engage in learning, we can readily see the extent to which they engage with the tasks, the kinds of responses they make, and the kinds of outcomes they produce. Children provide us with ample evidence of their growing abilities—in their talk, in their questions, in their reading and writing, in their behavior in different activities. Since we interact with the children in large groups, small groups, and individually, we are able to observe them in a variety of situations so that our assessments are based on multiple observations from multiple perspectives, not just one-shot, paper-and-pencil performance. Much of this evidence we take in and use immediately—for example, to provide a further explanation, a recommendation for switching activities, perhaps a probe. Some of it we jot down on sticky labels or Post-it notes and later put them in the anecdotal records we keep on each child (Figure 5–1). We observe social, emotional, and physical development as well as content-area growth. (Teachers who find this too daunting a task may find it easier to keep up with observing and making records on three children per day, writing up observations after the children have left for the day.)

To help us make sense of the daily information we are gathering on the children and to put it into a slightly broader perspective, we've developed a checklist that describes what seem to us to be the important milestones and attributes (see Appendix A). We have tried to keep this checklist relatively short so that we don't end up checking off a thousand tiny skills, which would defeat the whole purpose of the exercise. The categories on our checklist parallel the goals of the program. Cognitive development is divided into three areas: understanding of the world (social studies/science), numeracy (math), and literacy (reading, writing, listening, speaking). Aesthetic development covers literature, music, art, and drama. Social/emotional

11/14 Conference

 — Mom concerned about Merissa vying for
attention and competing with older brother (1st grader)
 — Mom thinks Merissa has low self esteem
 — I will ask Joan (counselor) to phone mom
with suggestions
 — was in previous school for only 1 month before
coming here

1/18

 — much more outgoing
 — very interested in books, has some sight vocab.
 — made several friends
 — chooses literacy activities during Choice Time

2/20

 — has become very comfortable, is even being silly
and chatting with others on rug during group time
 — is writing frequently, some traditional spelling
 — enjoys playdough lately
 — never chooses blocks
 — talks to me freely

3/16
 — understands adding and asks me to make
"adding papers" for her during Choice Time

12/14   uses initial consonants to read morning
    message

2/9   spends alot of time playing puppets
    with Sara and Lauren

3/11   read 3 Sunshine books to me during R+K

4/14   wrote morning message on her own,
    plays school alot

4/18   started crying today because she had
    been excluded by some other girls — they
    resolved it and things appear to be
    back to normal

FIGURE 5–1   Anecdotal Record for Merissa

development and physical development are assessed in a narrative form rather than in a checklist because it doesn't seem to us that there are milestones or specific attributes characteristic of development in these areas.

Early in the Fall, we sit down with each child and try to gather information about their developmental level. Throughout the year we have informal, individual conferences periodically with each child to assess specific areas on the checklist (letter recognition, sound-symbol associations, counting objects, simple addition, and so on) that we might have missed during our observations.

Periodically, we go over the checklist and record the progress made by individual children, drawing upon our daily observations and samples of the children's work. In this way, we maintain a current record of the progress being made by each child. We make a mental or written note of who needs special attention in certain areas. Keeping this information in mind, we engage with these children in activities that provide appropriate individual instruction. If Jared has trouble with handwriting, we need to take the time to show him how to form the letters and give him time to practice. If Brian does not settle with a book during Relax and Read, we might pair him up with someone who does. At the same time, we are sensitive to the children's developmental level—we wouldn't be providing this assistance if they weren't ready for it. We also use these records to help in our planning of future theme activities, to prepare for a conference with a parent, or occasionally to assist in a referral of a child to receive special services. These records are particularly helpful in writing reports at the end of each semester.

Writing books are an important source of information about a child's emergent literacy. When we review their writing samples we can determine their stage of development in reading, writing, drawing, and handwriting. For example, it is easy to see when a child has learned that print represents language or begins to use initial or ending sounds in writing. Because we save each child's writing books until the end of the year, we have an ongoing record of their growth and development during the year.

Summative Evaluation

Like all kindergarten teachers, we have to let people outside our classroom know, on a regular basis, how the children are doing.

We have conferences with parents (in November); we have report cards (in January and June); the children have to take standardized achievement tests (in June); and we meet with first-grade teachers to assist with placement into first grade. We also compile a portfolio of each child's work, and send it home at the end of the year.

Conferences. In November we have a conference with each parent. During this conference we ask the parents for their initial impressions of kindergarten. This gives us insight into their concerns and provides a meaningful focus to the conference. We tell parents how we view their child's development so far and discuss our concerns. We feel that parents appreciate our honesty if we express ourselves in a tactful manner. Parents have a wealth of knowledge about their children that should not be overlooked. This conference is essential in learning more about each child. (By the way, we always give ourselves a few minutes between conferences, to write down our thoughts and parents' comments. Otherwise, in the flurry of conferences, it's easy to forget what transpired.)

Meetings can be requested by a parent or teacher at any time the need arises. These are important ways of keeping the lines of communication open. We find this prevents a situation where problems are neglected or allowed to get out of control.

Report Cards. The report card we use is fairly general and is divided into five major areas: social and emotional development; work habits; large and small motor; math; reading; and writing. There is also an area for written comments that we find most useful—it allows us to speak more directly to the progress each child has made and mention strengths and attributes that aren't included on the report card. (Ideally, the report to parents should reflect the philosophy of the program, but in most schools there are differing philosophies and one report card unfortunately cannot reflect them all.) We send a note with the report card asking the parents to take some time to talk to their child about the report card. We don't want them to use the information in the report as a basis for punishment but rather as an opportunity for parents to talk with their children about their progress in school.

Standardized Achievement Tests. Our children are required to take standardized achievement tests for kindergartners. The information is used to gather statistics for the district and to identify children needing special programs in first grade.

Placing kindergartners in first grade. At the end of the year, we summarize all the information we have accumulated, and we pass this along to the first-grade teachers.

Portfolios. We save handwriting samples, spontaneous notes written by the children to us, drawings (including self-portraits done in September and June), anecdotal records, communications with parents, and any other relevant information. These are used as the basis for starting a portfolio for each child. In some schools, portfolios travel with the child through the grades. In our classroom, the portfolio is sent home with the child at the end of the kindergarten year.

Program Evaluation

We evaluate the effectiveness of our program in a number of ways: we send out questionnaires to four or five parents following each theme, asking them to let us know what their children learned from the themes, if they found the themes interesting and worthwhile, and if it prompted activity or discussion at home (see Appendix B). At conference times, we ask parents for their comments and reactions to the program. We also regularly monitor the reactions of the children themselves and make adjustments to the program (adding, changing, or discontinuing) accordingly.

At the end of the year, we send home a letter inviting parents to comment on the entire program. We take these comments very seriously and make adjustments to the program if we feel it is warranted.

Using the tools we have described (observations, anecdotal records, checklists, portfolios, report cards, standardized tests, theme and program evaluations), we are able to determine with some confidence the extent to which we have met our goals.

Appendix A
Evaluation Checklist

DATE	NOTES	ATTRIBUTE
Cognitive Development: **Understanding of the World** **(Social Studies/Science)**		
		• participates in Show-and-Tell
		• contributes to theme-related discussions
		• sometimes chooses theme-related activities during Choice Time
		• sometimes chooses theme-related book during Relax and Read
		• enjoys theme-related activities
		• is using the vocabulary associated with themes
		• had a special interest in the following themes (list)
		• notes on knowledge of social studies
		• notes on knowledge of science
Numeracy (Math)		
		• recognizes numbers 1–10
		• recognizes numbers 10–20
		• recognizes numbers beyond 20
		• can count by rote 1–15

DATE	NOTES	ATTRIBUTE
Numeracy (continued)		
		• can count by rote 1–30
		• uses one-to-one correspondence
		• can create sets 1–10
		• can create sets 10–20
		• understands simple addition
		• understands simple subtraction
		• understands concept "greater"
		• understands concept "less"
Literacy (Reading, writing, listening, speaking)		
		• participates in shared book experiences
		• enjoys listening to stories
		• holds book right side up
		• "reads" from front to back
		• "reads" from left to right
		• makes up story while looking at a book
		• retells story after having heard it
		• points to words while reading
		• settles with a book during Relax and Read
		• sometimes chooses book at Choice Time
		• recognizes names of most classmates

DATE	NOTES	ATTRIBUTE
Literacy (continued)		
		• identifies uppercase letters
		• identifies lowercase letters
		• has begun to use cueing systems • does it sound like language? (syntactic) • does it make sense? (semantic) • initial/final consonants (graphophonic)
		• uses picture clues
		• recognizes differences between • letters • words • sentences
		• expresses ideas and thoughts so others understand
		• writes own name
		• chooses only to draw pictures
		• scribble writing
		• writes random letters
		• has begun to use initial consonant sounds
		• has begun to use final consonant sounds
		• uses more than initial/final consonants
		• uses some traditional spelling
		• writes in sentences
		• can read own writing
		• uses writing in play

DATE	NOTES	ATTRIBUTE
	Aesthetic Development (Literature, Music and Movement, Art, Drama)	
		• enjoys stories from different genres
		• participates enthusiastically in literature activities
		• participates enthusiastically in music and movement activities
		• participates enthusiastically in art activities
		• participates enthusiastically in drama activities
		• sometimes chooses aesthetic activities at Choice Time
	Social/Emotional Development	
	Physical Development	

Appendix B
Theme Evaluation

Dear Parent:

As part of the evaluation of our kindergarten themes, we will be sending home a questionnaire to a few parents at the end of each theme. You will be receiving one of these questionnaires about once every six weeks.

Your help in assessing the effectiveness of the themes will be greatly appreciated.

Please answer the questions below and return to us as soon as possible.

Thank you,
Bonnie Walmsley
Anne Marie Camp

	YES	NO
1. Were you aware of the theme on _____?	☐	☐
2. Did your child show interest in the theme?	☐	☐
3. Did your child learn factual information?	☐	☐
4. Was your child motivated to learn more about the topic at home?	☐	☐
5. Did your child share poems, songs, stories, and related projects with you?	☐	☐

Additional Comments:

Appendix C
An annotated bibliography of useful sources

Blenkin, Geva M., & Kelly, A.V. (1981). *The primary curriculum.* London: Harper & Row.

    This book presents a theoretical and philosophical rationale for the progressive primary curriculum in the United Kingdom. It's a powerful and persuasive book that reminds us that the kind of approach we take in our book has a long tradition in both England and in the United States, and isn't to be treated as a new fad.

Bredekamp, Sue. (1987). *Developmentally appropriate practice in early childhood programs serving children from birth through age 8.* Washington, DC: National Association for the Education of Young Children.

    This book lays out NAEYC's beliefs about what is developmentally appropriate and what is not. The book is divided into three different age groups and is an invaluable reference for those working with children up to the age of eight. (This book is a must for those in charge of a school's early childhood programs or those working on curriculum at this level.)

Cambourne, Brian. (1988). *The whole story: Natural learning and the acquisition of literacy in the classroom.* New York: Scholastic.

    Cambourne feels that most teachers are prisoners of an outdated model of learning. He presents an alternative approach, based on eight "conditions" of learning. He argues that literacy learning should be as natural as learning to speak. This book is essential reading for those who want to understand the theory behind a developmentally-appropriate, whole-language approach to literacy teaching.

Fisher, Bobbi. (1991). *Joyful learning: A whole language kindergarten.* Portsmouth, NH: Heinemann.

Fisher explains how she organizes her whole-language kindergarten. She provides specific details that will be very helpful to a teacher trying to start her own whole-language kindergarten. The book includes all areas of the curriculum and is very practical.

Katz, Lilian G., & Chard, Sylvia C. (1989). *Engaging children's minds: The project approach.* Norwood, NJ: Ablex.

This book is based on work done in a British primary school, where project work is very popular. (Projects are in-depth studies of particular topics that one or more children undertake.) The book explains how to teach through project work, and it provides a well-reasoned theoretical rationale for projects.

Morrow, Leslie Mandel. (1989). *Literacy development in the early years.* Englewood Cliffs, NJ: Prentice-Hall.

This book is helpful to teachers, parents, college students, and administrators. It's a readable blend of theory and practice and a wonderful resource on early literacy. We highly recommend this book to anyone working with or studying young children.

Morrow, Lesley Mandel, & Smith, Jeffrey K. (1990). *Assessment for instruction in early literacy.* Englewood Cliffs, NJ: Prentice Hall.

This book is the most up-to-date collection of articles on measurement issues we can find. It is also one of the best, and we will be using many of its ideas in the coming years, as we continue to refine and develop our own kindergarten assessment techniques. The authors deal with both theoretical and practical issues in early literacy assessment.

Newman, Judith. (1984). *The craft of children's writing.* Portsmouth, NH: Heinemann.

This is a short and practical book on early writing. It contains many samples of children's writing to illustrate Judith Newman's points.

Peck, J.T., McCaig, G., & Sapp, M.E. (1988). *Kindergarten policies: What is best for children?* Washington, DC: National Association for the Education of Young Children.

> This book addresses some of the important and controversial issues that face kindergarten teachers, such as entry age, tests for screening, diagnosis, and readiness measurement. It also lays out the components of a developmentally appropriate curriculum. This is an excellent book to start with, and it is essential reading for all kindergarten teachers. (It will also introduce teachers to the NAEYC, and the many benefits of membership.)

Raines, Shirley C., & Canady, Robert J. (1990). *The whole language kindergarten.* NY: Teachers College Press.

> This is a new book that probably is intended as a college text, but it is so readable and contains so many practical suggestions that it will certainly have broad appeal to both college students and early childhood educators. Raines and Canady aim their book at traditional kindergarten teachers who are attracted to whole language but aren't sure how to make the transition. The book gives numerous practical examples, and it covers all areas of the curriculum. It's an excellent addition to a kindergarten professional library.

Schickedanz, Judith A. (1986). *More than the ABCs: The early stages of reading and writing.* Washington, DC: National Association for the Education of Young Children.

> This book explains literacy development from birth to the school years. It includes many practical suggestions for nurturing literacy development. This is a good book to recommend to parents who want to increase their own knowledge of emergent and beginning literacy.

Strickland, Dorothy, & Morrow, Lesley Mandel. (Eds.). (1989). *Emerging literacy: Young children begin to read and write.* Newark, DE: International Reading Association.

> This book is a collection of articles written by leading educators in the emergent literacy field. The articles are informative and practical and address many of the concerns that early childhood education teachers have. We recommend this book for all kindergarten teachers.

References

Baskwill, J., & Whitman, P. (1986). *The whole language source-book: A guide for teachers of grades one and two*. Richmond Hill, Ontario: Scholastic-TAB Publications..

Blenkin, G. M., & Kelly, A. V. (1981). *The primary curriculum*. London: Harper & Row.

Bradley Commission on History in Schools. (1988). *Building a history curriculum: Guidelines for teaching history in schools*. Washington, DC: Educational Excellence Network.

Bredekamp, S. (Ed.). (1987). *Developmentally appropriate practice in early childhood programs serving children from birth through age 8* (Expanded ed.). Washington, DC: National Association for the Education of Young Children.

Brown, R. (1973). *A first language: The early stages*. Cambridge, MA: Harvard University Press.

Burke, A. (1923). *A conduct curriculum for the kindergarten and first grade*. New York: Charles Scribner's Sons.

Cambourne, B. (1988). *The whole story: Natural learning and the acquisition of literacy in the classroom*. New York: Scholastic.

Cambourne, B., & Turbill, J. (1990). Assessment in whole-language classrooms: Theory into practice. *Elementary School Journal, 90*(3), 337–349.

Clay, M. M. (1972). *Reading: The patterning of complex behaviour*. Auckland, NZ: Heinemann.

Crabtree, C. (1989). History is for children. *American Educator, 13*(4), 34–39.

de Villiers, P. A., & de Villiers, J. G. (1979). *Early language.* Cambridge, MA: Harvard University Press.

Dewey, J. (1938). *Experience and education.* New York: Macmillan.

Gamberg, R., Kwak, W., Hutchings, M., & Altheim, J. (1988). *Learning and loving it: Theme studies in the classroom.* Portsmouth, NH: Heinemann.

Gesell, A. L. (1925). *The mental growth of the pre-school child.* New York: Macmillan.

Ginsburg, M. (1972). *The chick and the duckling.* New York: Macmillan.

Goodman, K. S., Goodman, Y. M., & Hood, W. J. (1989). *The whole language evaluation book.* Portsmouth, NH: Heinemann.

Graves, D. H. (1983). *Writing: Teachers and children at work.* Portsmouth, NH: Heinemann.

Gray, W. S. (1927). Training and experiences that prepare for reading. *Childhood Education, 3*, 213.

Greene, L., & Adeyanju, M. (1991). Exercise and fitness guidelines for elementary and middle school children. *Elementary School Journal, 91*(5), 437–444.

Haggitt, E. M. (1975). *Projects in the primary school.* London: Longman.

Hainstock, E. (1986). *Essential Montessori.* New York: New American Library.

Holdaway, D. (1979). *The foundations of literacy.* Sydney, Australia: Ashton-Scholastic.

Huck, C., Hepler, S., & Hickman, J. (1987). *Children's literature in the elementary school,* (4th ed.). New York: Holt.

Ilg, F. L., & Ames, L. B. (1972). *School readiness.* New York: Harper & Row.

Katz, L.G., & Chard, S.C. (1989). *Engaging children's minds: The project approach.* Norwood, NJ: Albex.

Krackowizer, A. M. (1919). *Projects in the primary grades: A plan of work for the primary grades and kindergarten.* Philadelphia: J. B. Lippincott.

Kraus-Boelte, M. (1876). *Characteristics of Froebel's method, Kindergarten training.* Paper read before the National Educational Association, Baltimore, July 10th, 1876.

Lilley, I. M. (1967). *Friederich Froebel: A selection from his writings.* Cambridge, England: Cambridge University Press.

Maeroff, G. I. (1992). Focusing on urban education in Britain. *Phi Delta Kappan, 73*(5), 352–358.

Martin, A. (1990). Social studies in kindergarten: A case study. *Elementary School Journal, 90*(3), 305–317.

McGill-Franzen, A. (in press). *Shaping the preschool agenda: Early literacy, public policy and professional beliefs.* Albany: State University of New York Press.

Moffett, J. (1967). *Teaching the universe of discourse.* Boston: Houghton Mifflin.

Moffett, J., & Wagner, B. J. (1983). *Student-centered language arts and reading, K–13: A handbook for teachers.* Boston: Houghton Mifflin.

Montessori, M. (1964). *The Montessori method.* New York: Schocken Books.

Morrow, L. M. (1989). *Literacy development in the early years.* Englewood Cliffs, NJ: Prentice Hall.

Morrow, L. M., & Smith, J. K. (1990). *Assessment for instruction in early literacy.* Englewood Cliffs, NJ: Prentice Hall.

Parker, F. W. (1894/1969). *Talks on pedagogics: An outline of the theory of concentration.* New York: Arno Press & *The New York Times.*

Peck, J. T., McCaig, G., & Sapp, M. E. (1988). *Kindergarten policies: What is best for children?* Washington, DC: National Association for the Education of Young Children.

Piaget, J. (1973). *To understand is to invent.* New York: Grossman.

Raines, S. C., & Canady, R. J. (1990). *The whole language kindergarten.* New York: Teachers College Press.

Rambusch, N. M. (1962). *Learning how to learn: An American approach to Montessori.* Baltimore, MD: Helicon Press.

Read, C. (1975). *Children's categorization of speech sounds in English.* Urbana, IL: National Council of Teachers of English.

Read, C. (1986). *Children's creative spelling.* London: Routledge & Kegan Paul.

Robinson, S. L. (1987). Kindergarten in America: Five major trends. *Phi Delta Kappan, 68,* 529–530.

Robison, H. F., & Spodek, B. (1965). *New directions in the kindergarten.* New York: Teachers College Press.

Ross, E. D. (1976). *The kindergarten crusade: The establishment of preschool education in the United States.* Athens, OH: Ohio University Press.

Schickedanz, J. A. (1986). *More than the ABCs: The early stages of reading and writing.* Washington, DC: National Association for the Education of Young Children.

Selsam, M.E. (1946). *Egg to chick.* New York: Harper & Row.

Shepard, L. A., & Smith, M. L. (Eds.). (1989). *Flunking grades: Research and policies on retention.* Philadelphia: Falmer.

Smith, F. (1988). *Understanding reading.* Hillsdale, NJ: Erlbaum.

Smith, L. E. W. (1972). *Toward a new English curriculum.* London: Dent.

Spodek, B. (1982). The kindergarten: A retrospective and contemporary view. In L. Katz (Ed.), *Current topics in early childhood education* (pp. 173–191). Norwood, NJ: Ablex.

Strickland, D., & Morrow, L. (Eds.). (1989). *Emerging literacy: Young children begin to read and write.* (pp. 135–146). Newark, DE: International Reading Association.

Strickland, D. S. (1989). A model for change: Framework for an emergent literacy curriculum. In D. S. Strickland & L. M. Morrow (Eds.), *Emerging literacy: Young children learn to read and write* (pp. 135–146). Newark, DE: International Reading Association.

Teale, W. H., & Sulzby, E. (Eds.). (1986). *Emergent literacy: Writing and reading.* Norwood, NJ: Ablex.

Tierney, R. J., Carter, M. A., & Desai, L. E. (1991). *Portfolio assessment in the reading-writing classroom.* Norwood, MA: Christopher Gordon Publishers.

Walmsley, S. A. & Walp, T. P. (1990). Integrating literature and composing into the language arts curriculum: Philosophy and practice. *Elementary School Journal, 90* (3), 251–74.

Weber, E. (1969). *The kindergarten: Its encounter with educational thought in America.* New York: Teachers College Press.